Balanced Horizons

How to Start and Grow Your Business as an Influencer

Our guidebooks offer no secret shortcuts or magic success formulas. Instead, they provide practical, manageable steps for achieving your goals. Through honest advice and actionable strategies, we empower you to take control of your journey, fostering steady progress towards your dreams, one step at a time.

How to Start and Grow Your Business as an Influencer

How to Start and Grow Your Business as an Influencer

Balanced Horizons

Contents

Section 1: Understanding Influencer Business

1.1 Defining Influencer Marketing

Influencer marketing is a form of social media marketing that uses endorsements and product mentions from influencers—individuals who have a dedicated social following and are viewed as experts within their niche. Influencer marketing works because of the high amount of trust that influencers have built up with their following, and recommendations from them serve as a form of social proof to their potential customers.

Influencer marketing can involve collaborations such as sponsored posts, reviews, takeovers, giveaways, and affiliate marketing, where influencers promote a product or service to their audience in exchange for payment or other benefits.

Influencer marketing can be categorized into different types, based on the number of followers an influencer has:

1. **Nano-influencers**: These influencers have fewer than 1,000 followers but tend to have a strong connection with their audience. They often focus on a very specific niche.
2. **Micro-influencers**: These influencers have between 1,000 and 100,000 followers. Like nano-influencers, they usually have a strong connection with their audience and a specific area of expertise.
3. **Macro-influencers**: These influencers have between 100,000 and 1 million followers. They have a wider reach than nano- and micro-influencers, but their engagement rate can be lower.
4. **Mega-influencers and celebrities**: These influencers have over 1 million followers. They have a massive reach, but their engagement rate tends to be the lowest.

Influencer marketing is a rapidly growing field, as businesses recognize the value of reaching consumers through trusted and relevant voices. It's particularly effective for reaching younger demographics, who tend to be sceptical of traditional advertising but are heavily engaged on social media.

1.2 The Rise of Influencer Culture

The rise of influencer culture is largely a product of the digital and social media age. As social media platforms like Instagram, YouTube, and TikTok have grown in popularity, they have provided a platform for individuals to share their interests, expertise, and lifestyles with a wider audience. This has led to the rise of influencers—individuals who have amassed a significant following and can sway the opinions, tastes, and purchasing decisions of their audience.

There are several reasons for the rise of influencer culture:

Shift in Media Consumption: Traditional forms of media such as newspapers and television have given way to digital platforms. Consumers, particularly younger demographics, are spending more time on social media and less time consuming traditional media.

Authenticity and Trust: Influencers often seem a sense of more genuine and relatable than traditional celebrities. They build their followings around their personal stories, interests, and lifestyles, which can create a sense of authenticity and trust with their audience.

Niche Interests: Influencers often focus on specific niches, from beauty and fashion to fitness, travel, cooking, and more. This allows them to build a dedicated and engaged following of individuals who share their interests.

Accessibility and Engagement: Social media allows influencers to engage directly with their audience, creating a sense of connection and accessibility. Followers can comment, like, and share posts, and influencers often respond, creating a dialogue that is not possible with traditional celebrities.

The Democratization of Fame: Social media has democratized fame, making it possible for anyone with a unique voice, talent, or perspective to build a following. This has resulted in a diverse array of influencers, from all walks of life.

The Success of Influencer Marketing: As businesses have seen success with influencer marketing, they have invested more into it, which has further fuelled the growth of influencer culture.

The rise of influencer culture has had a significant impact on marketing, consumer behaviour, and even societal norms, and it is likely to continue evolving as new platforms and trends emerge.

1.3 The Benefits and Opportunities of Being an Influencer

Being an influencer comes with a variety of benefits and opportunities, many of which are tied to the unique relationship that influencers have with their followers. Here are some of the key advantages:

Creative Freedom: Influencers often have the freedom to express themselves creatively, sharing their passions, interests, and ideas with their followers. This can be very fulfilling, particularly for influencers who are passionate about their niche.

Flexible Lifestyle: Many influencers can work from anywhere, set their own hours, and design their own lifestyle. This flexibility can be particularly appealing in today's digital, on-the-go society.

Earning Potential: Influencers can earn money through a variety of streams, such as sponsored posts, brand collaborations, affiliate marketing, merchandise, and more. Top influencers can earn significant income, although it is important to note that income can vary widely depending on factors like niche, audience size, engagement, and monetization strategy.

Opportunities for Collaboration: Influencers often have opportunities to collaborate with brands, other influencers, and media outlets. These collaborations can be mutually beneficial, providing exposure and opportunities for growth.

Building a Personal Brand: Being an influencer allows individuals to build their personal brand. This can open doors to other opportunities, such as speaking engagements, book deals, and even launching their own products or businesses.

Making a Difference: Influencers often have a platform to raise awareness about causes they care about, and they can make a positive impact in their communities or even globally.

Learning and Growth: Being an influencer involves constantly learning and adapting, as social media trends evolve quickly. This can lead to personal and professional growth.

It is important to note that being an influencer also comes with challenges and responsibilities. Influencers need to maintain authenticity while navigating brand partnerships, manage their time and business effectively, and deal with issues like privacy concerns and online criticism. Despite these challenges, many influencers find the benefits and opportunities make it a rewarding path.

1.4 The Challenges and Realities of Influencer Business

While being an influencer can offer many benefits and opportunities, it also comes with its share of challenges and realities. Here are some of the key considerations:

1. **Maintaining Authenticity**: Balancing sponsored content with authentic, personal content can be a challenge. Audiences value authenticity and can be turned off by content that feels too promotional or out of sync with the influencer's usual content.

2. **Building and Retaining an Audience**: Growing a follower base takes time and consistent effort. The influencer must continually engage with their audience and produce quality content to retain their interest and attract new followers.

3. **Dealing with Negative Feedback or Trolls**: Being in the public eye exposes influencers to criticism and negativity, which can sometimes be harsh or even abusive. Learning to manage and respond to such feedback is a significant challenge.

4. **Privacy Concerns**: Being an influencer often involves sharing aspects of one's personal life, which can lead to privacy concerns. Striking a balance between being relatable and maintaining personal privacy can be tricky.

5. **Income Instability**: The income of an influencer can be unpredictable and fluctuates based on factors like number of sponsorships, viewer engagement, platform algorithms, etc. It can also take considerable time to start earning a significant income.

6. **Platform Dependency**: The influencer's career is tied to the social media platforms they use. Any changes in these platforms' algorithms, policies, or popularity can impact their reach and engagement.

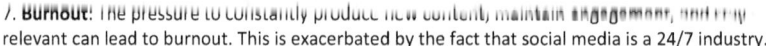

7. **Burnout**: The pressure to constantly produce new content, maintain engagement, and stay relevant can lead to burnout. This is exacerbated by the fact that social media is a 24/7 industry.

8. **Regulatory Compliance**: Influencers must be aware of and comply with relevant advertising and disclosure regulations, which can be complex and vary by country.

Despite these challenges, many influencers find their work rewarding and fulfilling. However, it is important for anyone considering this path to go into it with a clear understanding of both the opportunities and the realities of the influencer business.

Section 2: Discovering Your Niche

2.1 Identifying Your Passion and Expertise

Identifying your passion and expertise is a crucial step in discovering your niche, especially if you are planning to become an influencer. Here is a step-by-step guide to help you through the process:

1. **Self-Reflection**: Take some time to reflect on what you genuinely enjoy doing. What are the activities or topics that you could spend hours on without getting bored? What makes you feel energized, fulfilled, or excited? These could be potential areas of passion for you.

2. **Skills and Knowledge Assessment**: What are you good at? What areas do you excel in, both professionally and personally? Do you have any qualifications or experiences that set you apart from others? Reflect on your education, job history, hobbies, and any other experiences that have given you a unique set of skills or knowledge.

3. Feedback from Others: Sometimes, others can provide valuable insights into areas where we excel but may not recognize. Ask friends, family, colleagues, or mentors what they see as your strengths or talents.

4. **Journaling**: Consider keeping a journal to track your thoughts, feelings, and experiences related to various activities and topics. Over time, patterns may emerge that point to your passions and areas of expertise.

5. **Try New Things**: Experiment with new activities, topics, and experiences. Sometimes, you may not know if you are passionate about something or good at it until you give it a try.

6. **Find the Intersection**: Once you have identified potential passions and areas of expertise, look for where these overlap. This intersection could be your niche as an influencer.

7. **Test Your Passion and Expertise**: Before fully committing to a niche, test your passion and expertise. You can start by creating content on your chosen topic and gauge the response and engagement it receives. This will not only help you verify your choice but also start building your presence in your chosen niche.

Remember, your passion and expertise might evolve over time. Stay open to learning, growing, and adapting as you progress on your journey.

2.2 Researching and Analysing Market Trends

Keeping abreast of market trends is essential in the ever-evolving digital landscape. Whether you are an influencer looking to stay ahead or a business owner trying to stay competitive, understanding the current market trends can help you make informed decisions. Here is a step-by-step guide on how to research and analyse market trends:

1. **Identify Your Objective**: Start by understanding what you need from your research. Are you looking for emerging trends in your industry? Do you want to understand your audience better? Clear objectives will guide your research.

2. **Monitor Industry News**: Stay updated with industry-related news. Subscribe to industry newsletters, follow relevant blogs, podcasts, webinars, and join industry-specific forums or social media groups.

3. **Use Trend Tracking Tools**: Various online tools can help you identify and monitor trends. Google Trends, for instance, shows how often a term is searched for over a particular period. Other tools like SEMrush, Ahrefs, or BuzzSumo can also help identify trending topics.

4. **Social Media Listening**: Social media platforms are a goldmine for trend spotting. Keep an eye on trending hashtags, topics, or challenges across platforms like Instagram, Twitter, TikTok, and Facebook. Tools like Hootsuite, Sprout Social, or Mention can automate this process.

5. **Survey Your Audience**: Conducting surveys can provide direct insights into what your audience is interested in or their pain points. Tools like SurveyMonkey, Google Forms, or Typeform can help with this.

6. **Competitor Analysis**: Keep an eye on what your competitors or similar influencers in your niche are doing. Are they focusing on a new topic? Have they started using a new platform?

7. **Market Research Reports**: Companies like Nielsen, Ipsos, Statista, or Pew Research often publish market research reports that can provide valuable insights into larger industry trends.

8. **Attend Industry Events**: Trade shows, webinars, conferences, or industry meetups are great places to identify emerging trends and network with other professionals in your field.

9. **Analyse Data**: Once you've gathered information, analyse it to identify patterns or trends. Look for trends that align with your brand and can be incorporated into your strategy.

10. **Apply Your Findings**: After identifying a trend, consider how it can be applied to your strategy. Keep in mind, not every trend will be relevant to your brand or audience. It's important to be selective and choose trends that align with your brand identity and will resonate with your audience.

Remember, trends can change quickly, especially in the digital world, so continuous monitoring and adaptability are key.

2.3 Assessing Your Target Audience

Understanding your target audience is crucial for any influencer, as it guides the content you create, the tone and language you use, the social media platforms you focus on, and the brands with which you might collaborate. Here's a step-by-step guide to help you assess your target audience:

1. **Define Your Audience**: Start by creating a general profile of your target audience. Consider demographic information such as age, gender, location, and occupation. Also consider psychographic factors like interests, values, and attitudes.

2. **Analyse Your Existing Audience**: Use the analytics tools provided by social media platforms to learn about the people who are currently engaging with your content. Look at their demographics, when they are most active, and what content they engage with the most.

3. **Social Listening**: Pay attention to the conversations your audience is having online. What topics are they interested in? What are their pain points? Social listening can provide valuable insights into your audience's needs and preferences.

4. **Conduct Surveys**: Surveys can be a direct way to gather information about your audience. Ask them about their interests, preferences, and what they like about your content. Tools like SurveyMonkey, Google Forms, or Typeform can help with this.

5. **Create Audience Personas**: Based on your research, create audience personas - detailed descriptions of different segments of your audience. This can help you tailor your content to meet the needs and interests of these different segments.

6. **Monitor Engagement**: Pay attention to which posts get the most likes, comments, shares, and saves. This can give you an idea of what type of content resonates most with your audience.

7. **Competitor Analysis**: Look at the audiences of similar influencers or competitors. What content do they respond to? Are there gaps that you could fill?

8. **Ongoing Assessment**: Assessing your audience should be an ongoing process. As you grow and evolve as an influencer, your audience may also change. Regularly check your analytics and engage with your audience to keep up with their evolving needs and interests.

Remember, understanding your audience allows you to create content that resonates with them, which can lead to higher engagement and more meaningful interactions.

2.4 Choosing the Right Social Media Platforms

Choosing the right social media platforms for your influencer journey is crucial. Each platform has its unique characteristics, demographics, and content styles. Here's a step-by-step guide to help you make the right choice:

1. **Understand Each Platform's Strengths and User Demographics**: Every platform has its strengths and caters to a specific demographic. For example, Instagram is great for visually focused content and has a younger demographic, LinkedIn is perfect for professional and business-related content, TikTok is popular among Gen Z users with its short-form video content, while Facebook has a broad user base and multiple types of content.

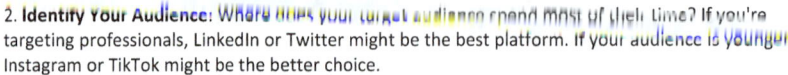

2. **Identify Your Audience**: Where does your target audience spend most of their time? If you're targeting professionals, LinkedIn or Twitter might be the best platform. If your audience is younger, Instagram or TikTok might be the better choice.

3. **Assess Your Content Type**: What type of content will you create? If you're a visual artist or a lifestyle influencer, Instagram or Pinterest could be ideal. If you're planning to create video content, consider YouTube or TikTok.

4. **Analyse Your Competitors**: Where are similar influencers or competitors in your niche most active? Observing their social media usage can give you insight into what might work best for you.

5. **Consider Your Personal Preferences**: Which platforms do you enjoy using the most? Being an influencer will require you to spend a significant amount of time on the platform, so it's essential to choose one that you find intuitive and enjoyable.

6. **Start Small and Expand Later**: It's better to start with one or two platforms and focus on building your presence there before expanding to other platforms. Spreading yourself too thin across multiple platforms can dilute your efforts.

7. **Experiment and Evaluate**: Once you've chosen a platform, experiment with different types of content, posting times, and engagement strategies. Monitor your analytics to see what works and what doesn't and adjust your strategy accordingly.

Remember, there's no one-size-fits-all answer when it comes to choosing the right social media platforms. It's about finding the best fit for your content, audience, and personal preferences.

Defining your brand identity as an influencer is a crucial step in setting yourself apart from the crowd and creating a consistent, recognizable presence across all your platforms. Here's a step-by-step guide to help you through the process:

1. Identify Your Core Values: What are the principles and beliefs that guide your actions? These values will become the foundation of your brand identity. For example, if you value authenticity, this could translate into being open and honest in your content.

2. Define Your Mission: What's the purpose of your brand? What do you want to achieve as an influencer? This mission will guide your decision-making and help you create a consistent brand.

3. Understand Your Audience: Who are you trying to reach? What are their interests, pain points, and aspirations? Understanding your audience will help you create a brand identity that resonates with them.

4. Determine Your Unique Selling Proposition (USP): What makes you unique or different from other influencers in your niche? This could be your unique perspective, your style, your expertise, or your approach to content.

5. Develop Your Brand Personality: Your brand personality is the human characteristics associated with your brand. Are you funny, serious, inspirational, adventurous, or friendly? This personality should come across in your content and interactions.

6. Create a Consistent Visual Identity: This includes elements like a logo, colour palette, typography, and any other visual elements that will be associated with your brand. These should be consistent across all your platforms.

7. Craft Your Brand Voice: Your brand voice is how your brand communicates with your audience. It should reflect your brand personality and be consistent across all your content and communication.

8. Build a Brand Story: A brand story is a cohesive narrative that encompasses the facts and feelings associated with your brand. It gives your audience a way to connect with you on an emotional level.

9. Stay Consistent: Once you've defined your brand identity, it's important to stay consistent. This helps build trust and recognition with your audience.

Remember, your brand identity is not static. It can evolve over time as you grow and as your audience's needs change. It's a good idea to periodically review your brand identity to make sure it's still serving you and your audience effectively.

Creating an authentic online persona is critical for an influencer. It's the essence of building trust and forming a genuine connection with your audience. Here are some steps to help you create an authentic online persona:

1. Be True to Yourself: The foundation of an authentic online persona is being true to yourself. Share your genuine thoughts, feelings, and experiences. If you try to be someone you're not, it can lead to inconsistency and eventually lose the trust of your audience.

2. Share Your Story: People connect with stories. Sharing your personal journey, including your successes and failures, can help your audience relate to you on a deeper level.

3. Show Vulnerability: Nobody's perfect. It's okay to show vulnerability and share your struggles. This not only makes you more relatable but also helps others who might be going through similar situations.

4. Engage with Your Audience: Don't just talk at your audience, engage with them. Respond to comments, ask for their opinions, and show appreciation for their support. This can foster a sense of community and make your audience feel valued.

5. Be Transparent: Honesty and transparency are key to maintaining trust. If you're promoting a product or service, be upfront about it. If you make a mistake, own up to it and apologize.

6. Stay Consistent: Consistency in your message and behaviour reinforces your authenticity. This doesn't mean you can't evolve or change your mind about something, but sudden, unexplained shifts in behaviour or opinion can confuse your audience and damage your authenticity.

7. Practice Empathy: Show understanding and empathy towards your audience. Acknowledge their struggles, celebrate their wins, and provide support when you can.

8. Respect Boundaries: While being open and authentic is important, remember to respect your own boundaries. You don't have to share everything. Decide what areas of your life you're comfortable sharing and what should remain private.

9. Continuous Learning and Growth: An authentic online persona isn't static. Strive for continuous learning and growth and share your journey with your audience.

Remember, authenticity is about being genuine and real. It's about showing up as your true self and building meaningful connections with your audience. It might take time to find your authentic voice, but it's worth the effort.

3.3 Crafting a Compelling Brand Story

Crafting a compelling brand story is an essential part of your influencer brand strategy. It is the narrative that connects you to your audience, sets you apart from other influencers, and gives your brand a unique voice. Here's a guide on how to craft your brand story:

1. Understand Your Audience: Your brand story needs to resonate with your audience. Understand their needs, interests, aspirations, and challenges to create a story that speaks to them.

2. Define Your 'Why': Simon Sinek, a renowned leadership expert, emphasizes starting with 'why.' Why did you become an influencer? What's your purpose or mission? This forms the backbone of your story.

3. Share Your Journey: How did you get to where you are now? Share the milestones, successes, and failures that led you to this point. Your journey humanizes your brand and makes it relatable.

4. Highlight Your Values: What principles guide your actions? How do these values influence your content and interactions with your audience? Highlighting these values can help you connect with like-minded individuals.

5. Showcase Your Unique Selling Proposition (USP): What sets you apart from other influencers in your niche? Your USP could be your unique perspective, your style, your expertise, or your approach to content.

6. Incorporate Testimonials and Reviews: If you've worked with brands or have received positive feedback from your followers, weave these into your story to build credibility and trust.

7. Create an Emotional Connection: Stories that evoke emotion are more memorable and impactful. Use emotion in your story to create a deeper connection with your audience.

8. Keep It Authentic: Authenticity is key in storytelling. Be truthful and honest. Don't exaggerate or make up stories that aren't true to your experience.

9. Make It Evolving: Your brand story is not set in stone. It should evolve as you grow and learn. Update your story as significant events or shifts occur in your journey.

10. Communicate Your Story Consistently: Once you've crafted your story, weave it into all your content and communication. It could be in your social media bio, in your video introductions, or in the captions of your posts.

Remember, a compelling brand story is more than just a timeline of events. It's a narrative that embodies your values, showcases your uniqueness, and creates an emotional connection with your audience.

Establishing your brand voice and values is a critical step in defining your identity as an influencer. Your brand voice is how you communicate with your audience, while your values guide your decisions and actions. Here's a guide on how to establish them:

1. Define Your Values: Start by identifying the principles and beliefs that are important to you. These could be things like authenticity, creativity, empathy, inclusivity, or sustainability. Your values should guide your actions, the content you create, the brands you choose to partner with, and how you interact with your followers.

2. Understand Your Audience: Your brand voice should resonate with your audience. Get to know their interests, values, and the language they use. This doesn't mean you should mimic them, but your voice should be relatable to them.

3. Develop Your Brand Personality: Your brand personality is the set of human characteristics associated with your brand. Are you funny, serious, inspirational, adventurous, or friendly? These characteristics should be reflected in your brand voice.

4. Craft Your Brand Voice: Based on your values, audience, and brand personality, craft your brand voice. It could be casual and friendly, authoritative, and informative, inspirational, and uplifting, or a mix. Your brand voice should be consistent across all platforms and types of content.

5. Create a Brand Voice Chart: A brand voice chart can help you maintain consistency. It lists the key attributes of your brand voice, with do's and don'ts for each attribute. For example, if one attribute is 'friendly', the do's might include using conversational language, and the don'ts might include avoiding jargon.

6. Align Your Actions with Your Values: It's not enough to just talk about your values, you need to live them. Make sure your actions, both online and offline, align with your values. If you value authenticity, be open and genuine in your content. If you value sustainability, only partner with brands that are eco-friendly.

7. Communicate Your Values: Let your audience know about your values. You can communicate them through your content, your bio, and your interactions with your audience.

8. Review and Evolve: As you grow and learn, your brand voice and values might evolve. Regularly review them to ensure they still align with who you are and who your audience is.

Remember, your brand voice and values are key elements of your brand identity. They set you apart from other influencers and help you build a genuine connection with your audience.

Section 4: Content Creation Strategies
4.1 Understanding the Importance of Quality Content

Quality content is one of the most essential elements in successful content creation, especially in the realm of influencer marketing. It plays a significant role in attracting, engaging, and retaining an audience, establishing credibility, and driving results. Below are some reasons why quality content is so important:

1. Attracts and Engages Audience: High-quality content can capture the attention of your target audience, engage them effectively, and keep them coming back for more. It can make your content stand out in the crowded digital landscape.

2. Builds Trust and Credibility: Quality content can help establish you as a credible, trustworthy source of information in your niche. This can increase your audience's confidence in you and make them more likely to value your opinions and recommendations.

3. Drives Engagement: Quality content encourages more likes, shares, comments, and other forms of engagement. This can help you build a strong, interactive community around your brand.

4. Improves SEO: Search engines reward quality content. Producing high-quality content can improve your search engine rankings, making it easier for new audiences to discover you.

5. Encourages Audience Retention: Consistently delivering high-quality content can help retain your audience over time. It can increase your audience's loyalty and turn them into long-term followers or customers.

6. Supports Your Brand Image: The quality of your content reflects on your brand. High-quality content can enhance your brand image and strengthen your overall brand identity.

7. Drives Conversions: Quality content can influence your audience's purchasing decisions, leading to higher conversion rates. It can make your promotional efforts more effective and increase your return on investment.

8. Enhances User Experience: Quality content, coupled with good design and easy navigation, enhances user experience. A positive user experience can increase your audience's satisfaction and make them more likely to recommend you to others.

Remember, quality over quantity is the key. It's better to produce fewer pieces of high-quality content than to churn out lots of low-quality content. Invest time and effort into creating content that provides value to your audience, aligns with your brand identity, and helps you achieve your goals.

Developing a content strategy and an editorial calendar is a fundamental part of being an influencer. These tools will help you to stay organized, consistent, and aligned with your goals. Here's a guide on how to develop them:

1. Define Your Content Goals: Start by identifying what you want to achieve with your content. This could be increasing your follower count, boosting engagement, driving traffic to a website, or promoting a product or service. Your goals should align with your overall influencer objectives.

2. Understand Your Audience: Research your audience to understand their interests, needs, and content consumption habits. This will help you create content that resonates with them.

3. Identify Content Types and Themes: Based on your goals and audience, decide on the types of content you will create (e.g., blog posts, videos, photos, stories) and the themes or topics they will cover. This should align with your niche and brand identity.

4. Decide on Content Frequency and Timing: How often will you post content, and when? Consider your audience's habits (when they are most active) and your capacity to create quality content.

5. Create an Editorial Calendar: An editorial calendar is a schedule of when and what you will post. It can help you plan ahead, stay organized, and maintain consistency. You can create an editorial calendar using tools like Google Calendar, Asana, or specialized software like CoSchedule.

6. Plan for Engagement: Your strategy should also include how you will engage with your audience. This could be responding to comments, hosting Q&As, or creating interactive content like polls or quizzes.

7. Monitor and Adjust: Once you start implementing your content strategy, monitor your performance against your goals. Use analytics to understand what's working and what's not, and adjust your strategy as needed.

8. Include Key Events or Dates: Make sure to include important dates in your editorial calendar. This could be holidays, events in your niche, product launches, or any date that is significant for your brand or audience.

9. Plan for Content Creation and Curation: Your strategy should include a mix of created (original) and curated (shared from other sources) content. Make sure to plan time for both.

10. Diversify Your Content: Diversify your content to keep your audience engaged. This could mean varying your content formats, themes, or posting times.

Remember, a content strategy and editorial calendar is not set in stone. It should be flexible and evolve as your brand grows and changes. Regularly review and update it to ensure it continues to serve your needs and helps you achieve your goals.

4.3 Creating Engaging and Shareable Content

Creating engaging and shareable content is crucial for growing your online presence as an influencer. Here are some steps to guide you through this process:

1. Understand Your Audience: Know what type of content your audience finds interesting, useful, and shareable. Use insights from your social media analytics to understand their interests, demographics, and behaviours.

2. Create High-Quality Content: Quality matters more than quantity. Make sure your content is well-produced, visually appealing, and provides value to your audience.

3. Be Authentic: Authenticity resonates with audiences. Be true to your personality and beliefs and let them shine through your content.

4. Make It Relatable: Content that resonates on a personal level is more likely to be shared. Tell stories, share experiences, and tap into emotions.

5. Incorporate Visuals: Images, videos, infographics, and other visual content are more engaging and shareable than text alone.

6. Encourage Interaction: Ask questions, include calls-to-action, and create interactive content like polls or quizzes to encourage your audience to engage with your content.

7. Use Hashtags and Keywords: Hashtags and keywords make your content discoverable to a wider audience. Use popular and relevant hashtags, but don't overdo it.

8. Stay Relevant: Stay up-to-date with trends and current events in your niche. Create content around trending topics to increase its shareability.

9. Collaborate with Other Influencers: Collaborations can help you reach a larger audience. Plus, content featuring multiple influencers is often more engaging and shareable.

10. Provide Value: Whether it's educational, entertaining, or inspiring, make sure your content provides value. Content that offers something valuable is more likely to be shared.

11. Timing is Important: Post your content when your audience is most active. Use your social media analytics to identify the best times.

12. Test and Analyse: Regularly review your analytics to see what types of content get the most engagement and shares and adjust your content strategy accordingly.

Creating engaging and shareable content is both an art and a science. It requires creativity, understanding of your audience, and continuous learning and adjustment based on analytics and feedback.

Leveraging different content formats can help diversify your content, cater to different audience preferences, and increase your overall reach and engagement. Here's a guide on how to use various content formats:

1. Images: Visuals are vital in social media, and images are among the most straightforward formats to utilize. Use high-quality, eye-catching images that tell a story or convey a message. Infographics are another type of image content that can be highly engaging and informative.

2. Videos: Videos are highly engaging and can be used to convey complex ideas in an easily digestible format. There are various types of video content you can create, such as tutorials, product reviews, vlogs, interviews, and live videos.

3. Text Posts: Text posts, such as status updates, tweets, or captions, are essential for communicating with your audience. Make your text posts engaging and relatable, and don't forget to engage with followers who comment.

4. Stories (Instagram, Facebook, Snapchat): Stories are short, temporary pieces of content that allow for a more casual and personal form of interaction. You can use them for behind-the-scenes content, polls, Q&As, and more.

5. Blogs: If you have a website or a blog, long-form content can help establish your authority in your field. Blog posts can be informative, opinion-based, or personal narratives.

6. Podcasts: If you're comfortable speaking, a podcast can be a powerful content format to leverage. Podcasts allow you to connect with your audience on a more intimate level and provide them with valuable audio content. Here's how you can make the most of podcasts:

1. Choose a Relevant Topic: Select a topic that aligns with your niche, expertise, and audience's interests. Ensure it's something you're passionate about and can consistently produce content on.

2. Plan Your Episodes: Outline the structure and content of each episode. Consider having a mix of solo episodes, interviews with guests, or panel discussions. Create a content calendar to stay organized.

3. Invest in Quality Equipment: Use a good-quality microphone, headphones, and audio editing software to ensure clear and professional sound. Listeners appreciate high-quality audio.

4. Create Engaging Content: Make your podcast informative, entertaining, and engaging. Use storytelling techniques, provide actionable advice, share personal anecdotes, and ask thought-provoking questions.

5. Promote Your Podcast: Create eye-catching cover art and optimize your podcast title and description for discoverability. Promote your podcast on your social media platforms, website, and through collaborations with other influencers.

6. Submit to Podcast Directories: Submit your podcast to popular directories like Apple Podcasts, Spotify, Google Podcasts, and Stitcher. This will make it easily accessible to a broader audience.

7. Encourage Reviews and Subscriptions: Ask your listeners to leave reviews and ratings on podcast directories. Positive reviews can attract more listeners and help your podcast gain visibility.

8. Engage with Your Audience: Encourage listener feedback and interaction. Respond to comments, messages, and emails. Consider incorporating a segment where you answer listener questions or feature their stories.

9. Collaborate with Guests: Invite experts, influencers, or industry leaders as guests on your podcast. This not only adds credibility but also exposes your podcast to their audience, potentially expanding your reach.

10. Cross-Promote: Leverage your other content platforms to promote your podcast. Share snippets or highlight episodes on social media, embed episodes on your website, and mention your podcast in blog posts or videos.

11. E-books: If you have in-depth knowledge on a specific topic, consider creating e-books or digital guides. These can be downloadable resources that provide valuable information to your audience.

12. Interviews: Conducting interviews with experts or other influencers in your niche can bring fresh perspectives and valuable insights to your audience. It also helps you build connections and expand your network.

13. Case Studies: Share real-life examples or case studies that demonstrate the effectiveness of a product, strategy, or approach. This helps build credibility and shows the practical application of your expertise.

14. Templates and Worksheets: Provide downloadable templates or worksheets that your audience can use to simplify tasks, organize information, or achieve specific goals. This practical content can be highly valuable and shareable.

15. Web Series: Create a series of videos or episodes focused on a particular theme or topic. This allows you to dive deeper into subjects and engage your audience over an extended period.

16. Interactive Quizzes or Polls: Engage your audience with interactive content, such as quizzes or polls, which allows them to participate and share their opinions. This fosters interaction and increases the likelihood of sharing.

17. Behind-the-Scenes Content: Share glimpses into your daily life, work process, or creative journey. This humanizes your brand and makes your audience feel more connected to you.

18. Reviews and Recommendations: Share your thoughts and experiences on products, services, books, or other resources related to your niche. Honest and well-informed reviews can be valuable to your audience and encourage sharing.

19. Guest Contributions: Collaborate with other influencers or experts in your niche by featuring guest contributions on your blog or social media platforms. This brings fresh perspectives and exposes your audience to new voices.

20. Memes and Humorous Content: Infuse humour and memes into your content when appropriate. This can resonate with your audience, make them laugh, and encourage sharing.

Remember to analyse your audience's preferences, monitor engagement metrics, and adapt your content strategy accordingly. Diversifying your content formats keeps your audience engaged and allows you to cater to different preferences and platforms.

Building an engaged and loyal fan base is crucial for long-term success as an influencer. Here are some strategies to help you cultivate a dedicated community:

1. Consistently Provide Value: Create content that educates, entertains, or inspires your audience. Consistently delivering high-quality content that resonates with them will keep them engaged and coming back for more.

2. Engage and Respond: Actively engage with your audience by responding to comments, messages, and inquiries. Show genuine interest in their opinions, questions, and feedback. This fosters a sense of connection and makes them feel valued.

3. Be Authentic: Stay true to yourself and maintain authenticity in your content and interactions. People are more likely to connect with and support someone who is genuine and relatable.

4. Build a Community: Encourage interaction and create a sense of community among your followers. This can be done through live sessions, creating Facebook groups or forums, hosting virtual events, or promoting user-generated content. Encourage your fans to engage with each other and foster a supportive environment.

5. Offer Exclusive Content or Benefits: Provide your loyal fans with exclusive access to content, special discounts, or behind-the-scenes insights. This makes them feel appreciated and gives them a reason to stay engaged and connected.

6. Collaborate with Your Audience: Involve your fans in your content creation process. Seek their input on topics, ideas, or decisions. This empowers them and makes them feel like valued contributors.

7. Utilize Multiple Channels: Engage with your audience across various platforms, such as social media, email newsletters, blogs, podcasts, or YouTube channels. This allows you to reach them where they prefer to consume content and strengthens your overall presence.

8. Host Giveaways or Contests: Organize giveaways or contests that require engagement from your audience, such as sharing, tagging friends, or creating user-generated content. This encourages participation and helps expand your reach.

9. Show Appreciation: Regularly express gratitude to your fans for their support. This can be through shout outs, features, or even personalized messages. Make them feel valued and recognized for their contribution to your journey.

10. Continuously Improve: Listen to your audience's feedback, adapt to their evolving needs, and continuously improve your content and engagement strategies. This shows your commitment to providing the best experience for your fans.

Building an engaged and loyal fan base takes time and consistent effort. Focus on fostering meaningful connections, providing value, and creating a positive community experience. Your dedicated fans will not only support you but also become advocates for your brand, helping you grow and expand your reach.

5.2 Effective Engagement and Community Building

Effective engagement and community building are crucial for nurturing a loyal and active audience as an influencer. Here are some strategies to help you engage with your followers and build a thriving community:

1. Be Responsive: Respond to comments, messages, and inquiries in a timely manner. Show genuine interest in your audience's thoughts, questions, and feedback. Engaging in conversations demonstrates that you value their input and fosters a sense of connection.

2. Initiate Conversations: Start meaningful conversations by asking questions, seeking opinions, or requesting feedback. Encourage your audience to share their experiences and engage with your content. This creates a sense of involvement and makes them feel heard.

3. Encourage User-Generated Content: Prompt your followers to create and share content related to your brand or niche. This could include challenges, contests, or themed photo/video submissions. Repost and give credit to those who participate, which encourages others to join in and builds a sense of community.

4. Create Exclusive Content for Your Community: Offer special content or benefits exclusively to your community members. This could be access to behind-the-scenes footage, exclusive tutorials, or early access to new products or promotions. This fosters a sense of belonging and provides value to your loyal followers.

5. Foster a Positive and Supportive Environment: Set the tone for your community by establishing guidelines that encourage respectful and constructive interactions. Moderate discussions to maintain a safe and inclusive space where everyone feels comfortable expressing their opinions.

6. Host Live Q&A Sessions and Virtual Events: Engage with your audience in real-time through live Q&A sessions, webinars, or virtual meetups. This allows for direct interaction, enables you to address their questions, and deepens the connection between you and your community.

7. Collaborate with Your Community: Involve your audience in your content creation process. Seek their input on topics, ask for suggestions, or involve them in decision-making. This empowers them and makes them feel like active participants in your journey.

8. Acknowledge and Celebrate Milestones: Recognize and celebrate important milestones, such as hitting follower milestones, anniversaries, or accomplishments. Give shoutouts or feature your community members who have achieved notable goals. This not only celebrates their success but also fosters a sense of pride and belonging within your community.

9. Consistency and Regular Engagement: Maintain a consistent presence by posting regularly and engaging with your community consistently. This shows your commitment to them and helps build anticipation and a sense of reliability.

10. Listen and Adapt: Pay attention to your community's feedback and preferences. Adapt your content, strategies, and offerings based on their needs and interests. Showing that you value their input and take their feedback into account strengthens the relationship between you and your audience.

Remember, building an engaged community takes time and effort. Stay authentic, be present, and provide value to your followers. By fostering a sense of belonging and actively engaging with your audience, you can create a vibrant and loyal community around your brand.

5.3 Collaborating with Other Influencers and Brands

Collaborating with other influencers and brands can be a powerful strategy to expand your reach, tap into new audiences, and create valuable content. Here are some tips for effective collaboration:

1. Define Your Objectives: Determine what you hope to achieve through collaboration. It could be reaching a new audience, gaining credibility, increasing engagement, or creating innovative content. Clearly define your objectives to guide your collaboration efforts.

2. Find Complementary Influencers/Brands: Look for influencers or brands that align with your values, target audience, and niche. Seek out those who complement your content and have a similar or overlapping audience. This ensures a more natural fit and higher chances of success.

3. Identify Common Goals: Collaborate with influencers or brands that share similar goals or have a shared mission. This helps create a cohesive narrative and aligns your efforts towards a common purpose.

4. Reach Out with a Personalized Pitch: When approaching potential collaborators, personalize your outreach. Highlight why you think collaboration would be beneficial for both parties and explain how you can create value together. Show that you've done your research and have a genuine interest in working with them.

5. Co-create Unique and Engaging Content: Brainstorm ideas together and create content that combines your unique perspectives and expertise. This could include joint videos, blog posts, podcasts, social media campaigns, or even events. The content should be engaging, relevant to both audiences, and showcase the strengths of each collaborator.

6. Leverage Cross-Promotion: Amplify your collaborative efforts by cross-promoting each other's content. Share and tag each other in posts, stories, and videos. This exposes your audience to your collaborator's brand and vice versa, expanding your reach and potential follower base.

7. Provide value to your collaborators: Think about what you can bring to the table and how you can provide value to your collaborators. It could be sharing your network, providing access to your audience, or offering unique resources. Mutual benefit is key to building successful collaborations.

8. Be Clear on Expectations: Clearly communicate your expectations and discuss the scope of the collaboration upfront. Discuss deliverables, timelines, and any financial arrangements if applicable. Setting clear expectations helps avoid misunderstandings and ensures a smooth collaboration process.

9. Foster Authentic Relationships: Build genuine relationships with your collaborators. Engage with their content, support their initiatives, and maintain open communication. Authentic connections often lead to long-term collaborations and mutual support.

10. Evaluate and Learn: After the collaboration, assess its impact and effectiveness. Analyse metrics, gather feedback, and reflect on what worked well and what could be improved. Use these insights to refine future collaborations and continue to grow.

Remember, collaboration should be mutually beneficial and authentic. Choose partners that align with your brand values and audience and create content that resonates with both parties' followers. By leveraging each other's strengths and audiences, you can amplify your impact and create valuable experiences for your collaborative efforts.

5.4 Harnessing the Power of User-Generated Content

Harnessing the power of user-generated content (UGC) can be a game-changer for your brand. It allows your audience to become active participants in creating and sharing content related to your brand, resulting in increased engagement, authenticity, and reach. Here's how you can effectively leverage UGC:

1. Encourage and Incentivize UGC: Prompt your audience to create and share content related to your brand by encouraging them through contests, challenges, or giveaways. Offer incentives like discounts, exclusive access, or the chance to be featured to motivate participation.

2. Create a Branded Hashtag: Establish a unique branded hashtag that your audience can use when posting UGC related to your brand. This makes it easy for you to discover and curate the content, as well as for others to find and engage with it.

3. Showcase UGC on Your Platforms: Highlight UGC on your social media platforms, website, or other marketing channels. Repost or share user-generated photos, videos, testimonials, or reviews. This not only recognizes and appreciates your audience but also encourages others to contribute.

4. Engage with UGC Creators: Show appreciation by engaging with the creators of UGC. Like, comment, and respond to their posts to foster a sense of connection and encourage ongoing participation.

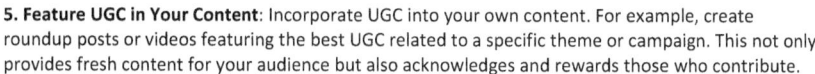

5. Feature UGC in Your Content: Incorporate UGC into your own content. For example, create roundup posts or videos featuring the best UGC related to a specific theme or campaign. This not only provides fresh content for your audience but also acknowledges and rewards those who contribute.

6. Request Permission and Give Credit: Always ask for permission before using someone's UGC and give proper credit. This demonstrates respect for the creator and helps build trust with your audience.

7. Leverage Stories and Testimonials: Use UGC stories and testimonials as social proof to build credibility and trust with your audience. Share how your products or services have positively impacted the lives of your customers, as shared through their UGC.

8. Collaborate with UGC Creators: Consider collaborating with UGC creators by featuring them in your content, partnering on projects, or hosting joint campaigns. This strengthens the bond with your audience and creates a sense of co-creation.

9. Monitor and Moderate UGC: Keep an eye on the UGC being shared about your brand. Moderate and respond to UGC appropriately, addressing any concerns or issues promptly. This ensures a positive and safe environment for everyone involved.

10. Share UGC Beyond Social Media: Extend the reach of UGC beyond social media. Incorporate UGC into your email newsletters, blog posts, or even offline marketing materials. This helps showcase the authenticity of your brand across various touchpoints.

Remember, when leveraging UGC, always prioritize authenticity, respect, and engagement. UGC allows your audience to become advocates for your brand and helps foster a strong sense of community. By showcasing and amplifying the content created by your audience, you can create a powerful and authentic connection with your customers.

As an influencer, there are various revenue streams you can explore to monetize your brand and content. Here are some common revenue streams for influencers:

1. Brand Collaborations/Sponsored Content: Partner with brands and create sponsored content in the form of sponsored posts, videos, or reviews. Brands pay you to promote their products or services to your audience.

2. Affiliate Marketing: Promote products or services through affiliate programs. You earn a commission for each sale or action generated through your unique affiliate links or codes.

3. Advertisements: Display ads on your website, blog, or YouTube channel. You can use ad networks like Google AdSense or work directly with brands for sponsored ads.

4. Merchandise and Products: Create and sell merchandise or branded products such as clothing, accessories, or digital products like e-books or courses. Your loyal audience can purchase these items, supporting you while showcasing their affiliation with your brand.

5. Brand Ambassadorships: Establish long-term partnerships as a brand ambassador for companies. This involves promoting their brand, products, or services over an extended period and often includes additional perks or benefits.

6. Events and Workshops: Host live events, workshops, or masterclasses where your audience can participate for a fee. This allows you to provide personalized experiences and share your expertise directly with your followers.

7. Speaking Engagements: Leverage your expertise and reputation to secure speaking engagements at conferences, industry events, or webinars. You can earn speaking fees while expanding your reach and establishing yourself as a thought leader.

8. Sponsored Travel and Experiences: Collaborate with travel brands, tourism boards, or hospitality companies to create sponsored travel content. This can involve sponsored trips, experiences, or accommodations, allowing you to share your adventures with your audience.

9. Patreon or Membership Platforms: Offer exclusive content, behind-the-scenes access, or special perks through membership platforms like Patreon. Your dedicated fans can support you by subscribing to these paid memberships.

10. Content Licensing: License your content, such as photos, videos, or written work, to brands, publishers, or media outlets. This allows them to use your content for their marketing campaigns, publications, or other purposes in exchange for licensing fees.

Remember, diversifying your revenue streams can provide stability and long-term income as an influencer. Choose the revenue streams that align with your brand and resonate with your audience.

It's essential to maintain authenticity and transparency throughout your monetization efforts to maintain trust with your audience.

6.2 Sponsored Content and Brand Partnerships

Sponsored content and brand partnerships are popular revenue streams for influencers. They involve collaborating with brands to create promotional content that aligns with your audience and brand values. Here's how to effectively engage in sponsored content and brand partnerships:

1. Define Your Target Audience and Niche: Clearly identify your target audience and niche. This will help you attract brands that are relevant to your audience and ensure a more authentic partnership.

2. Establish Your Brand Identity: Develop a strong and consistent brand identity that sets you apart from others. Brands look for influencers whose brand aligns with their own image and values.

3. Build an Engaged and Active Audience: Focus on growing and engaging your audience through valuable content and meaningful interactions. Brands are more likely to partner with influencers who have an engaged and loyal following.

4. Research and Select Brands Carefully: Thoroughly research brands before entering into partnerships. Ensure that the brand's values, products, and target audience align with yours. Choose brands that genuinely resonate with you and your audience.

5. Create a Media Kit: Develop a professional media kit that highlights your audience demographics, engagement rates, reach, previous brand collaborations, and other relevant metrics. This will provide brands with valuable information when considering a partnership.

6. Reach Out or Respond to Collaboration Opportunities: Actively seek out collaboration opportunities by reaching out to brands or responding to their partnership inquiries. Tailor your pitch to showcase how your content and audience can benefit the brand.

7. Negotiate Clear Terms and Deliverables: Clearly define the terms, expectations, and deliverables of the partnership. This includes the type and number of posts, compensation, timelines, exclusivity, and rights usage. A well-defined agreement helps ensure a smooth collaboration.

8. Maintain Authenticity: Stay true to your brand and maintain authenticity in your sponsored content. Your audience values your honesty, so it's important to disclose sponsored partnerships transparently and provide genuine opinions and experiences.

9. Create High-Quality and Engaging Content: Develop sponsored content that is engaging, visually appealing, and aligned with your usual content style. Focus on telling a compelling story and showcasing the brand's value to your audience.

10. Monitor and Report on Campaign Performance: Track the performance of your sponsored content using analytics and provide the brand with comprehensive reports. This helps demonstrate the success of the partnership and establishes trust for future collaborations.

Remember, it is important to strike a balance between sponsored and organic content. Overly promotional content can risk alienating your audience. Select partnerships that genuinely resonate with your audience and maintain the trust and connection you've built with them.

6.3 Affiliate Marketing and Sponsored Posts

Affiliate marketing and sponsored posts are two popular methods for influencers to monetize their platforms. Here's a breakdown of each:

Affiliate Marketing: Affiliate marketing involves promoting products or services and earning a commission for each sale or action made through your unique affiliate links or codes. Here's how to effectively leverage affiliate marketing:

1. **Choose Relevant Affiliate Programs**: Select affiliate programs that align with your niche and audience's interests. Look for reputable affiliate networks or individual brands that offer products or services your audience would find valuable.
2. **Disclose Your Affiliate Partnerships**: Be transparent with your audience by clearly disclosing your affiliate partnerships. It's important to maintain trust and transparency with your followers.
3. **Promote Products You Believe In**: Only promote products or services that you genuinely believe in and would recommend to your audience. Your authenticity and honest opinions are crucial for maintaining your credibility.
4. **Create Compelling Content**: Develop high-quality content that showcases the benefits and value of the products or services you're promoting. Use engaging visuals, personal experiences, and storytelling techniques to capture your audience's attention.
5. **Provide Value to Your Audience**: Focus on how the promoted products or services can solve a problem, fulfil a need, or enhance your audience's lives. Offer valuable insights, tips, or tutorials related to the promoted products to provide additional value.
6. **Track Performance and Optimize**: Monitor your affiliate marketing efforts to track conversions, clicks, and revenue. This data helps you understand what strategies and products are most effective, allowing you to optimize your promotions for better results.

Sponsored Posts: Sponsored posts involve collaborating with brands to create content that promotes their products or services. Here's how to approach sponsored posts effectively:

1. **Select Relevant and Authentic Partnerships**: Choose brand partnerships that align with your values, audience's interests, and brand image. Authenticity is key to maintaining the trust of your audience.
2. **Understand Brand Objectives**: Collaborate closely with the brand to understand their goals and desired outcomes for the sponsored post. This helps you create content that meets their expectations while still resonating with your audience.
3. **Create Engaging and Creative Content**: Develop sponsored posts that are visually appealing, engaging, and align with your usual content style. Incorporate the brand's messaging naturally into the post while maintaining your authentic voice.
4. **Be Transparent**: Clearly disclose that the post is sponsored to maintain transparency with your audience. Use appropriate disclosure language or hashtags as required by advertising regulations and guidelines.

5. **Showcase Genuine Product Benefits**: Highlight the unique selling points and benefits of the sponsored product or service. Share personal experiences, testimonials, or how the product has positively impacted your life to make the content more relatable.
6. **Monitor and Analyse Engagement**: Track the performance and engagement of your sponsored posts. Analyse metrics such as likes, comments, shares, and conversions to assess the effectiveness of the partnership and inform future collaborations.

Remember, whether it's affiliate marketing or sponsored posts, it's important to choose partnerships and products that align with your audience's interests and provide value. Strive for authenticity and transparency in your promotions to maintain the trust and engagement of your followers.

6.4 Creating and Selling Your Own Products or Services

Creating and selling your own products or services is a powerful way to monetize your influence and establish your brand. Here are the steps to successfully create and sell your own products or services:

1. Identify a Market Need: Research your target audience to identify gaps or needs that your product or service can fulfil. Understand their pain points, desires, and preferences to create something that resonates with them.

2. Define Your Product or Service: Based on your market research, determine what type of product or service you want to create. It could be physical products, digital products, online courses, consulting services, or any other offering that aligns with your expertise and audience.

3. Develop Your Unique Value Proposition: Determine what sets your product or service apart from competitors. Clearly communicate the unique value it provides and how it addresses your audience's needs or solves their problems.

4. Plan and Create Your Product or Service: Outline the features, specifications, and content for your offering. Depending on the type of product, you may need to design prototypes, create digital assets, record videos, or write content. Ensure your product or service meets high-quality standards.

5. Set a Competitive Price: Conduct market research to determine a competitive and profitable price for your product or service. Consider factors such as production costs, value delivered, audience affordability, and pricing strategies.

6. Build an E-commerce Platform: Set up an e-commerce platform to showcase and sell your products or services. This could be a website with an integrated shopping cart, a dedicated online store on platforms like Shopify, or utilizing third-party marketplaces like Etsy or Amazon.

7. Develop Marketing and Sales Strategies: Create a marketing plan to promote your products or services effectively. Utilize various marketing channels such as social media, email marketing, content marketing, paid advertising, and influencer collaborations to reach your target audience.

8. Build Trust and Social proof. Establish credibility and trust by leveraging social proof. Encourage customer reviews, testimonials, and case studies. Highlight success stories and customer satisfaction to build confidence in your offering.

9. Offer Excellent Customer Service: Provide exceptional customer service to build customer loyalty and positive word-of-mouth. Respond promptly to inquiries, address concerns, and exceed customer expectations. Positive experiences can lead to repeat purchases and referrals.

10. Continuously Improve and Innovate: Gather feedback from customers and use it to enhance your product or service. Continuously innovate and stay up-to-date with industry trends to ensure your offerings remain relevant and competitive.

Remember, creating and selling your own products or services requires thorough planning, quality execution, and effective marketing. Stay focused on delivering value to your customers and adapt your offerings based on feedback and market demands. With dedication and a customer-centric approach, you can build a profitable business around your own products or services.

Understanding advertising and disclosure regulations is crucial for influencers to maintain transparency, comply with legal requirements, and build trust with their audience. Here are some key aspects to consider:

1. Federal Trade Commission (FTC) Guidelines (United States): In the United States, the FTC provides guidelines that influencers must follow to ensure transparency in advertising. The key principles include:

- Disclosing Material Connections: Influencers must disclose any material connections they have with brands or advertisers, including financial arrangements, free products or services, or partnerships.
- Clear and Conspicuous Disclosures: Disclosures must be clear, prominent, and easily understood by the audience. They should be placed before any affiliate links or sponsored content, using explicit language like "ad," "sponsored," or "paid partnership."
- Honest and Genuine Recommendations: Influencers must provide honest opinions and recommendations about products or services, ensuring that their endorsements are truthful and not misleading.

2. Advertising Standards Authority (ASA) Guidelines (United Kingdom): In the United Kingdom, the ASA sets standards for influencer marketing to protect consumers. Key points include:

- Disclosure: Influencers must disclose their commercial relationships with brands clearly and prominently, using appropriate labels such as "ad," "sponsored," or "paid partnership."
- Misleading Content: Influencers should avoid creating content that could mislead consumers, ensuring that claims about products or services are accurate and substantiated.
- Identification of Ads: Advertisements must be clearly identifiable as such, ensuring that consumers can easily distinguish between advertising and editorial content.

3. Other Regional Regulations: Different countries have their own advertising and disclosure regulations. It's important for influencers to familiarize themselves with the guidelines specific to their region, such as the Competition Bureau (Canada), Advertising Standards Council (Australia), or Consumer Protection Law (Germany).

4. Social Media Platform Policies: Influencers should also be aware of the specific guidelines and policies of social media platforms they use. Platforms like Instagram, YouTube, and TikTok have their own rules regarding sponsored content disclosures, branded content tags, and paid partnership features.

5. Compliance and Best Practices:

- Clearly disclose sponsored content, paid partnerships, or affiliate links at the beginning of the post or video description to ensure transparency.

- Use appropriate hashtags or labels recommended by regulatory authorities or platforms.
- Avoid deceptive practices, false claims, or misleading information about products or services.
- Regularly review and update your understanding of advertising regulations to stay compliant.

It's essential to consult legal professionals or industry experts for specific advice regarding advertising and disclosure regulations in your region. Adhering to these regulations helps maintain transparency, protects your audience, and fosters trust in your brand.

7.2 Protecting Your Intellectual Property Rights

Protecting your intellectual property rights is crucial as an influencer to safeguard your original content and maintain ownership over your creative work. Here are some key steps to protect your intellectual property:

1. Copyright Your Content: Copyright law automatically grants you certain rights over your original content as soon as it is created. However, registering your copyright with the appropriate copyright office in your country provides additional legal protection and allows you to take legal action against infringement.

2. Watermark Your Content: Adding a visible watermark to your images, videos, or other creative works can deter unauthorized use or misuse of your content. Watermarks typically include your logo, name, or website URL and serve as a visual indication of your ownership.

3. Monitor and Enforce Your Rights: Regularly monitor the internet and social media platforms for any unauthorized use or infringement of your content. If you discover someone using your content without permission, take appropriate action to enforce your rights, such as issuing takedown notices or pursuing legal remedies if necessary.

4. Terms of Use and Licensing Agreements: Clearly state your terms of use and licensing agreements on your website or in your content. Specify how others may use your content, whether it's for personal use, non-commercial purposes, or with explicit permission. This helps establish guidelines for proper usage and provides a legal basis for enforcement.

5. Use Contracts for Collaborations: When collaborating with brands, agencies, or other influencers, use written contracts or agreements that outline the terms of the collaboration, including intellectual property rights. Clearly define the ownership of content, usage rights, and any limitations or restrictions.

6. Protect Trademarks and Brand Identity: Consider registering trademarks for your brand name, logo, or any other unique identifiers associated with your influencer persona. Trademark registration provides legal protection against unauthorized use or infringement by others.

7. Stay Informed and Seek Legal Advice: Stay updated on intellectual property laws and regulations in your jurisdiction. Consult with intellectual property lawyers or legal professionals experienced in digital content and influencer marketing to understand your rights, options, and the best strategies for protecting your intellectual property.

8. DMCA Takedown Notices: Familiarize yourself with the Digital Millennium Copyright Act (DMCA) if you operate in the United States. The DMCA provides a mechanism to request the removal of infringing content from online platforms or websites.

Remember, protecting your intellectual property is an ongoing process. Stay vigilant, document your original creations, and take appropriate action to enforce your rights when necessary. Seeking legal advice can provide valuable guidance tailored to your specific situation and jurisdiction.

7.3 Maintaining Ethical Practices and Transparency

Maintaining ethical practices and transparency is essential for influencers to build trust, credibility, and long-term relationships with their audience. Here are some key guidelines to follow:

1. Disclose Sponsored Content: Be transparent about any paid partnerships, sponsored posts, or brand collaborations. Clearly disclose when content is sponsored or when you have received compensation or free products. Use appropriate labels, such as "ad," "sponsored," or "paid partnership," and ensure they are easily visible to your audience.

2. Provide Honest and Genuine Recommendations: Ensure that your endorsements, reviews, or recommendations are honest, unbiased, and based on your genuine experiences and opinions. Avoid making false or misleading claims about products or services.

3. Respect Your Audience's Privacy: Obtain proper consent when using personal information or images of your audience. Respecting their privacy builds trust and maintains a positive relationship.

4. Maintain Transparency in Affiliate Marketing: Clearly disclose your participation in affiliate marketing and the use of affiliate links or codes. Let your audience know that you may earn a commission from their purchases through your affiliate links.

5. Verify the Accuracy of Information: Before sharing any news, statistics, or factual information, verify their accuracy from reliable sources. Avoid spreading misinformation or unsubstantiated claims.

6. Avoid Unfair Competition: Conduct your business ethically and avoid engaging in unfair competition practices, such as defamation, false advertising, or undermining competitors. Focus on delivering value and maintaining integrity.

7. Respect Copyright and Intellectual Property: Ensure that you have the necessary rights or permissions before using copyrighted material, such as images, music, or videos. Give proper credit to the original creators and respect intellectual property rights.

8. Engage Authentically with Your Audience: Foster genuine connections with your audience by engaging in meaningful conversations, responding to comments and messages, and valuing their feedback. Avoid using automated or impersonal responses.

9. Be Transparent in Collaborations: Clearly communicate the nature and terms of your collaborations or partnerships with brands, agencies, or other influencers. Maintain integrity by only endorsing products or services that align with your values and that you genuinely believe in.

10. Regularly Review and Update Your Practices: Stay informed about ethical guidelines, regulations, and industry best practices. Continuously review and update your practices to ensure they align with evolving standards and expectations.

By adhering to ethical practices and maintaining transparency, you can foster trust and credibility with your audience. Your commitment to honesty, integrity, and authenticity will help you build a loyal following and establish a positive reputation as an influencer.

Scaling your influencer business involves expanding your reach, increasing your revenue, and leveraging opportunities for growth. Here are some strategies to help you scale your influencer business:

1. Define Your Growth Objectives: Clearly define your growth objectives and set specific goals. This could include increasing your audience size, diversifying your revenue streams, expanding your partnerships, or entering new markets. Having clear objectives will guide your decision-making and focus your efforts.

2. Develop a Scalable Content Strategy: Create a scalable content strategy that allows you to consistently deliver high-quality content to your audience. Identify content formats that resonate with your audience and can be produced efficiently. Consider repurposing content, batching tasks, or outsourcing certain aspects to increase productivity.

3. Collaborate with Other Influencers and Brands: Seek collaborations with other influencers and brands to amplify your reach and tap into new audiences. Collaborations can include joint content creation, cross-promotion, or co-branded campaigns. Choose partners who align with your brand values and have a complementary audience.

4. Expand Your Digital Presence: Explore new social media platforms, channels, or formats to expand your digital presence. Consider creating a podcast, launching a YouTube channel, or exploring emerging platforms to reach new audiences and diversify your content offerings.

5. Invest in Professional Branding and Design: Enhance your brand's visual identity and professionalism by investing in high-quality branding, design, and photography. A cohesive and visually appealing brand presence can attract new followers, partnerships, and brand collaborations.

6. Build a Team or Outsource Tasks: As your business grows, consider building a team or outsourcing certain tasks to increase efficiency and productivity. This could involve hiring a virtual assistant, content creator, editor, or social media manager to help with content creation, scheduling, or administrative tasks.

7. Leverage Data and Analytics: Use data and analytics to gain insights into your audience, content performance, and growth opportunities. Analyse metrics such as engagement rates, audience demographics, and content reach to identify trends, optimize your strategies, and make informed decisions.

8. Diversify Your Revenue Streams: Explore additional revenue streams beyond brand collaborations, such as e-commerce, digital products, online courses, or consulting services. Diversifying your revenue sources can provide stability and increased earning potential.

9. Build Long Turm Partnerships: Cultivate long-term relationships with brands and agencies by consistently delivering value, maintaining professionalism, and exceeding expectations. Long-term partnerships can provide recurring collaborations and stable income.

10. Continuous Learning and Adaptation: Stay up-to-date with industry trends, changes in algorithms, and evolving best practices. Continuously learn and adapt your strategies to stay relevant, maximize opportunities, and overcome challenges in the influencer landscape.

Scaling your influencer business requires strategic planning, adaptability, and a focus on delivering value to your audience and partners. By implementing these strategies, you can expand your influence, increase your revenue, and take your influencer business to new heights.

8.2 Developing a Business Plan and Setting Goals

Developing a business plan and setting goals is a crucial step in building a successful influencer business. Here's a framework to help you develop your business plan and set achievable goals:

1. Executive Summary: Provide an overview of your influencer business, including your mission statement, target audience, unique value proposition, and key objectives.

2. Business Description: Describe your influencer business in detail, including your niche, content focus, platforms you operate on, and any unique features or services you offer. Highlight your competitive advantage and what sets you apart from others.

3. Market Analysis: Conduct a thorough analysis of your target market, including audience demographics, market trends, competitor analysis, and potential growth opportunities. Understand your audience's needs, preferences, and challenges to tailor your content and strategies accordingly.

4. Monetization Strategy: Outline your monetization strategies and revenue streams, such as brand collaborations, sponsored content, affiliate marketing, merchandise sales, or digital products. Describe how you plan to generate income from your influencer activities.

5. Content Strategy: Develop a content strategy that aligns with your brand and resonates with your target audience. Define your content themes, formats, frequency, and distribution channels. Consider how you will engage and grow your audience through valuable and consistent content.

6. Marketing and Promotion: Detail your marketing and promotion strategies to increase your visibility, attract new followers, and engage your existing audience. Include tactics such as social media advertising, search engine optimization (SEO), collaborations, email marketing, and content distribution.

7. Operations and Resources: Identify the resources, tools, and technologies you need to run your influencer business effectively. This includes equipment, software, team members (if applicable), and any third-party services you may require.

8. Financial Planning: Create a financial plan that outlines your budget, projected revenue, expenses, and profit margins. Consider factors such as production costs, marketing expenses, platform fees, taxes, and investments in growth.

9. Goal Setting: Set SMART goals (Specific, Measurable, Achievable, Relevant, and Time-bound) to track your progress and measure success. Define both short-term and long-term goals related to audience growth, engagement rates, revenue targets, partnerships, and any other key performance indicators (KPIs).

10. Evaluation and Review: Establish a process for regularly evaluating and reviewing your business plan and goals. Monitor your performance, track metrics, and make adjustments to your strategies as needed. Stay agile and responsive to changes in the influencer landscape and market conditions.

Remember, your business plan is a dynamic document that should evolve as your influencer business grows. Regularly revisit and update your plan to reflect new opportunities, challenges, and objectives. Having a well-defined business plan and clear goals will guide your actions, help you stay focused, and increase your chances of success in the influencer industry.

8.3 Managing Finances and Budgeting

Managing finances and budgeting effectively is crucial for the success and sustainability of your influencer business. Here are some key steps to help you manage your finances:

1. Track Income and Expenses: Keep a detailed record of your income and expenses related to your influencer business. Use accounting software, spreadsheets, or dedicated apps to track all financial transactions. Categorize expenses to gain insights into your spending patterns.

2. Set a Budget: Create a budget that outlines your projected income and anticipated expenses. Include fixed costs like equipment, subscriptions, and marketing expenses, as well as variable costs like production costs or travel expenses. Setting a budget helps you allocate funds wisely and make informed financial decisions.

3. Separate Business and Personal Finances: Open a separate bank account for your influencer business to ensure proper separation of business and personal finances. This simplifies financial management and provides clarity for tax purposes.

4. Tax Compliance: Understand your tax obligations and ensure compliance with local tax laws. Consult with a tax professional to determine the specific tax requirements for influencers in your jurisdiction. Keep track of deductible expenses and maintain organized records for tax purposes.

5. Establish an Emergency Fund: Set aside a portion of your earnings to build an emergency fund. Having a financial cushion helps you manage unexpected expenses or navigate periods of reduced income.

6. Monitor Cash Flow: Regularly review your cash flow to understand the timing of your income and expenses. Ensure you have sufficient funds to cover your expenses and maintain a healthy cash flow. Consider establishing payment terms with brands or clients to manage cash flow more effectively.

7. Evaluate and Optimize Expenses: Regularly evaluate your expenses and identify areas where you can optimize spending. Look for cost-saving opportunities, negotiate better deals with service providers, or explore alternative solutions that offer similar value at a lower cost.

8. Revenue Diversification: Explore opportunities to diversify your revenue streams beyond brand collaborations. Consider creating and selling digital products, offering consulting services, or leveraging affiliate marketing to generate additional income.

9. Plan for Growth and Investment: Allocate a portion of your earnings for business growth and investment. This can include investing in equipment upgrades, marketing campaigns, professional development, or hiring additional team members as your business expands.

10. Regular Financial Reviews: Conduct regular financial reviews to assess your progress, review your budget, and make adjustments as needed. Analyse your financial reports, track key metrics, and identify areas for improvement or growth opportunities.

By implementing effective financial management practices, you can maintain financial stability, make informed business decisions, and set yourself up for long-term success as an influencer. Consider consulting with a financial advisor or accountant to ensure you have a solid financial foundation and make the most of your earnings.

8.4 Building a Team and Outsourcing Tasks

As your influencer business grows, you may find it beneficial to build a team or outsource certain tasks to increase efficiency and focus on high-value activities. Here's a step-by-step guide to building a team and outsourcing tasks effectively:

1. Identify Areas for Outsourcing: Determine which tasks or responsibilities can be delegated to others. Common areas for outsourcing include content creation, video editing, graphic design, social media management, administrative tasks, customer support, and financial management. Assess your strengths and weaknesses to identify the tasks that are best suited for outsourcing.

2. Define Roles and Responsibilities: Clearly define the roles and responsibilities for the team members or freelancers you plan to bring on board. Create job descriptions that outline the specific tasks, skills required, and expectations for each role. This helps you identify the right candidates and set clear expectations from the start.

3. Determine the Hiring Model: Decide whether you want to hire permanent employees, work with freelancers or contractors, or utilize a combination of both. Consider factors such as budget, workload, and the need for specialized skills. Hiring freelancers can offer flexibility, while permanent employees provide long-term commitment and alignment with your brand.

4. Find and Vet Potential Candidates: Seek candidates through job boards, social media platforms, referrals, or freelancing websites. Evaluate their skills, experience, portfolio, and cultural fit with your brand. Conduct interviews or request work samples to assess their capabilities and professionalism.

5. On-board and Train Team Members: Once you've selected team members or freelancers, provide them with comprehensive onboarding and training. Familiarize them with your brand guidelines, content style, and expectations. Clearly communicate your goals, processes, and workflows to ensure everyone is aligned.

6. Establish Effective Communication Channels: Set up communication channels to facilitate smooth collaboration and feedback. This could include project management tools, instant messaging platforms, or regular team meetings. Clear and timely communication helps ensure tasks are executed effectively and everyone is on the same page.

7. Delegate and Empower: Delegate tasks to team members or freelancers, providing them with the necessary resources, information, and authority to complete their assigned responsibilities. Trust your team and empower them to make decisions within their designated areas.

8. Provide Feedback and Performance Evaluation: Regularly provide feedback and conduct performance evaluations to assess the effectiveness of your team members or freelancers. Recognize their achievements, address any concerns, and provide opportunities for growth and development.

9. Maintain Clear Documentation: Establish systems to document processes, guidelines, and brand standards. This ensures consistency and allows team members to reference the necessary information when needed. Documenting workflows also facilitates smooth transitions when team members change, or new members join.

10. Review and Adjust as Needed: Continuously review your team structure, workflows, and outsourcing arrangements. Assess their effectiveness and make adjustments as your business evolves. Be open to feedback and learn from any challenges or lessons along the way.

Building a team or outsourcing tasks can help you leverage the skills of others, increase productivity, and focus on strategic aspects of your influencer business. However, it's important to effectively manage and communicate with your team to maintain a cohesive and aligned approach.

Balancing work and personal life is crucial for maintaining overall well-being and avoiding burnout. Here are some strategies to help you achieve a better work-life balance as an influencer:

1. Set Boundaries: Establish clear boundaries between your work and personal life. Define specific working hours and designate personal time for relaxation, hobbies, and spending time with loved ones. Stick to these boundaries as much as possible to maintain a healthy balance.

2. Prioritize Self-Care: Make self-care a priority by incorporating activities that recharge and rejuvenate you into your routine. This can include exercise, meditation, reading, pursuing hobbies, or spending time outdoors. Taking care of your physical and mental well-being is essential for maintaining balance.

3. Plan and Organize: Use effective planning and organization techniques to optimize your time and tasks. Create a schedule or to-do list that includes both work-related and personal activities. Prioritize your tasks and allocate dedicated time for different activities to ensure a balanced approach.

4. Delegate and Outsource: As your influencer business grows, delegate tasks or outsource certain responsibilities to others. This can free up time for personal activities and alleviate some of the workload. Determine which tasks can be effectively handled by others and seek support when needed.

5. Learn to Say No: It's important to learn to say no to commitments or opportunities that may overwhelm you or encroach upon your personal time. Prioritize activities that align with your goals and values, and politely decline or delegate tasks that do not contribute to your well-being or professional growth.

6. Disconnect from Technology: Take regular breaks from technology and social media. Set specific periods of time where you disconnect from work-related notifications, emails, and social media platforms. Use this time to unwind, relax, and focus on personal activities without distractions.

7. Communicate with Your Loved Ones: Regularly communicate with your loved ones about your work schedule, commitments, and the importance of maintaining work-life balance. Seek their support and understanding and involve them in activities that promote quality time and connection.

8. Create a Dedicated Workspace: Establish a dedicated workspace that separates your work environment from your personal space. This helps create a psychological boundary between work and personal life, enabling better focus during work hours and better relaxation during personal time.

9. Take Regular Breaks: Incorporate regular breaks into your work routine. Short breaks throughout the day can improve productivity and focus. Also, plan for longer breaks, vacations, or time off to recharge and rejuvenate.

10. Regularly Assess and Adjust: Regularly assess your work-life balance and make adjustments as needed. Be mindful of any signs of burnout, stress, or imbalance and take proactive steps to address them. Flexibility and adaptability are key in maintaining a healthy work-life balance.

Remember, achieving work-life balance is an ongoing process that requires conscious effort and regular evaluation. It may not always be perfect, but by implementing these strategies and making your well-being a priority, you can find a healthier balance between your work as an influencer and your personal life.

9.2 Managing Stress and Burnout

Managing stress and preventing burnout is essential for maintaining your well-being and sustaining long-term success as an influencer. Here are some strategies to help you effectively manage stress and avoid burnout:

1. Recognize the Signs: Be aware of the signs and symptoms of stress and burnout, such as fatigue, decreased motivation, irritability, difficulty concentrating, and physical ailments. Recognizing these signs early can help you take proactive measures to manage stress.

2. Prioritize Self-Care: Make self-care a priority by engaging in activities that promote relaxation, rejuvenation, and physical and mental well-being. This can include exercise, meditation, getting enough sleep, maintaining a healthy diet, and pursuing hobbies or activities that bring you joy.

3. Set Realistic Expectations: Avoid overcommitting yourself and set realistic expectations for your workload and deliverables. Learn to say no to tasks or opportunities that may overwhelm you or jeopardize your well-being. Remember that quality is more important than quantity.

4. Establish Boundaries: Set clear boundaries between work and personal life. Define specific working hours and honour designated personal time for yourself and your loved ones. Avoid checking work-related emails or engaging in work activities during personal time.

5. Delegate and Outsource: Delegate tasks or outsource certain responsibilities to others, whether it's hiring assistants, content creators, or using automation tools. Offloading tasks can help reduce your workload and allow you to focus on high-value activities.

6. Take Regular Breaks: Incorporate regular breaks into your work schedule. Step away from your work, stretch, go for a walk, or engage in activities that help you recharge. Taking breaks can improve focus, productivity, and overall well-being.

7. Practice Stress Management Techniques: Explore stress management techniques such as deep breathing exercises, mindfulness meditation, journaling, or engaging in activities that promote relaxation and stress reduction. Find techniques that work for you and incorporate them into your routine.

8. Seek Support and Connection: Maintain a support network of friends, family, or fellow influencers who understand the challenges you face. Share your experiences, seek advice, and offer support to others. Connection and support can help alleviate stress and provide a sense of community.

9. Time Management and Prioritization: Effectively manage your time by prioritizing tasks, setting realistic deadlines, and breaking down big projects into manageable chunks. Use productivity tools and techniques to stay organized and focused.

10. Regularly Assess and Adjust: Regularly assess your stress levels and well-being. Be proactive in identifying potential stressors and adjusting your strategies as needed. Be open to seeking professional help or guidance if stress and burnout become overwhelming.

Remember, managing stress and preventing burnout is a continuous effort. It requires self-awareness, self-care, and a commitment to maintaining a healthy work-life balance. By implementing these strategies and being mindful of your well-being, you can thrive as an influencer while preserving your mental and physical health.

9.3 Cultivating a Growth Mindset

Cultivating a growth mindset is essential for personal and professional development as an influencer. It involves adopting a belief that skills, abilities, and intelligence can be developed through dedication, effort, and continuous learning. Here are some strategies to help you cultivate a growth mindset:

1. Embrace Challenges: View challenges as opportunities for growth rather than obstacles. Embrace them with a positive mindset, knowing that they provide valuable learning experiences and opportunities to develop new skills.

2. Persist in the Face of Setbacks: See setbacks as temporary and part of the learning process. Instead of giving up, view them as opportunities to learn, adapt, and improve. Embrace a "fail forward" mentality and use setbacks as steppingstones to future success.

3. Learn from Feedback: Embrace feedback, both positive and constructive, as a tool for growth. See it as an opportunity to gain insights, improve your skills, and refine your approach. Actively seek feedback from mentors, peers, and your audience to enhance your performance.

4. Adopt a Continuous Learning Mindset: Cultivate a love for learning and seek out opportunities to expand your knowledge and skills. Stay curious, explore new ideas, and actively seek out resources, courses, books, or workshops that can help you develop professionally.

5. Emphasize Effort and Process: Focus on the effort and process rather than solely on the outcome. Celebrate your progress, milestones, and the steps you take to improve. Embrace the journey and the incremental growth that comes with it.

6. Surround Yourself with Growth-Oriented Individuals: Surround yourself with individuals who have a growth mindset and who support your personal and professional development. Engage in

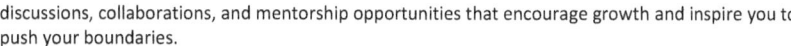

discussions, collaborations, and mentorship opportunities that encourage growth and inspire you to push your boundaries.

7. Practice Self-Reflection: Regularly engage in self-reflection to assess your strengths, areas for improvement, and goals. Set specific, measurable, attainable, relevant, and time-bound (SMART) goals and regularly monitor your progress. Adjust your strategies as needed to stay on track.

8. Embrace Challenges Outside Your Comfort Zone: Seek opportunities to step outside your comfort zone and take on new challenges. This helps expand your skill set, build resilience, and develop confidence in your ability to adapt and learn.

9. Focus on the Power of "Yet": Embrace the power of the word "yet" when facing challenges or setbacks. Instead of saying, "I can't do it," add "yet" to the end, such as "I can't do it yet, but I'm working on it." This small shift in mindset acknowledges that growth and improvement are ongoing processes.

10. Celebrate Growth and Progress: Acknowledge and celebrate your growth and progress along the way. Take time to reflect on your achievements, milestones, and the personal growth you've experienced. This positive reinforcement reinforces your belief in your ability to learn and grow.

Cultivating a growth mindset is a lifelong journey. Embrace the belief that you have the capacity to continuously improve, adapt, and excel in your influencer career. By embracing challenges, seeking feedback, and fostering a love for learning, you can cultivate a growth mindset that propels you towards success and fulfilment.

9.4 Practicing Self-care and Wellness

Practicing self-care and prioritizing wellness is essential for maintaining your overall well-being as an influencer. Here are some strategies to help you practice self-care and prioritize your wellness:

1. Prioritize Physical Health: Take care of your physical health by adopting healthy habits. Get regular exercise, eat a balanced diet, stay hydrated, and get enough sleep. Pay attention to your body's needs and be available for activities that promote physical well-being.

2. Manage Stress: Develop effective stress management techniques that work for you. This can include activities like meditation, deep breathing exercises, yoga, or engaging in hobbies that help you relax and unwind. Find healthy coping mechanisms to manage stress and prevent burnout.

3. Establish Boundaries: Set boundaries between work and personal life to create time and space for yourself. Designate specific times for work and leisure activities and avoid excessive multitasking. Disconnect from work-related activities during personal time to allow yourself to recharge and focus on self-care.

4. Unplug from Technology: Take regular breaks from technology and social media to reduce screen time and minimize digital distractions. Engage in offline activities that bring you joy, such as spending time in nature, reading, or practicing hobbies that don't involve screens.

5. **Practice Mindfulness** Incorporate mindfulness into your daily routine. Practice being present in the moment, observe your thoughts and emotions without judgment, and cultivate gratitude. Mindfulness can help reduce stress, increase self-awareness, and enhance overall well-being.

6. **Nurture Relationships:** Foster meaningful connections with loved ones and friends. Be available for social activities, engage in quality conversations, and prioritize spending time with those who bring positivity and support to your life.

7. **Engage in Hobbies and Recreation:** Set aside time for activities that bring you joy and allow you to recharge. Pursue hobbies, interests, or creative outlets that help you relax, express yourself, and find fulfilment outside of your work as an influencer.

8. **Seek Support:** Reach out for support when needed. Connect with a trusted friend, family member, or therapist who can provide guidance, lend an empathetic ear, and offer emotional support. Seeking professional help is not a sign of weakness but a proactive step towards self-care.

9. **Practice Gratitude:** Cultivate a mindset of gratitude by regularly acknowledging and appreciating the positive aspects of your life. Keep a gratitude journal or take time each day to reflect on things you are grateful for. This practice can enhance your overall well-being and mindset.

10. **Regularly Assess and Adjust:** Regularly assess your self-care routine and make adjustments as needed. Prioritize activities that truly nourish and rejuvenate you. Listen to your body and mind and adapt your self-care practices to best meet your changing needs.

Remember, self-care is a continuous practice that requires commitment and self-awareness. By prioritizing self-care and wellness, you'll be better equipped to navigate the demands of your influencer career, maintain balance, and sustain your overall well-being.

Conclusion:
Reflecting on Your Journey as an Influencer

Reflecting on your journey as an influencer is an important practice that can provide valuable insights, help you track your progress, and guide your future growth. Here are some key aspects to consider when reflecting on your journey:

1. Goals and Milestones: Review the goals you set for yourself as an influencer and assess how far you've come. Reflect on the milestones you've achieved along the way and celebrate your successes. Take note of the challenges you faced and how you overcame them.

2. Personal Growth: Reflect on how you have grown as an individual throughout your influencer journey. Consider the skills you've developed, the knowledge you've gained, and the lessons you've learned. Acknowledge your personal achievements and the areas in which you've evolved.

3. Content and Engagement: Evaluate your content strategy and its impact on your audience. Assess the engagement levels, feedback, and interactions you've received from your followers. Identify the types of content that resonated the most with your audience and the ones that might need improvement.

4. Brand Identity: Reflect on your brand identity and how it has evolved over time. Consider the values, messaging, and aesthetics that define your brand. Assess whether your brand identity aligns with your goals and audience expectations.

5. Collaborations and Partnerships: Evaluate the collaborations and partnerships you've had with brands, influencers, or other individuals. Reflect on the value and impact they brought to your influencer journey. Assess the partnerships that were successful and those that may require improvement or reconsideration.

6. Audience Insights: Analyse your audience demographics, engagement metrics, and feedback. Understand the preferences and interests of your audience to better tailor your content and engagement strategies. Consider conducting surveys or engaging in conversations with your audience to gather their insights and feedback.

7. Lessons Learned: Identify the lessons you've learned from both successes and setbacks. Reflect on the strategies and approaches that worked well for you and those that didn't. Consider how you can apply these lessons to improve your future endeavours as an influencer.

8. Future Aspirations: Consider your future aspirations as an influencer. Reflect on the direction you want to take your influencer career, the goals you want to achieve, and the impact you want to make. Set new goals and outline actionable steps to move forward.

9. Self-Reflection: Engage in regular self-reflection to assess your motivations, passion, and alignment with your influencer journey. Reflect on whether your journey is bringing you fulfilment and whether it aligns with your values and purpose.

10. **Adjustments and Growth:** Based on your reflections, make any necessary adjustments to your strategies, content, branding, or partnerships. Embrace growth opportunities and consider how you can continue evolving as an influencer.

Remember, reflection is an ongoing practice that should be incorporated into your influencer journey regularly. Use your reflections as a guide for continuous improvement, growth, and authenticity. Be open to feedback, remain adaptable, and stay connected with your audience to build a strong and impactful influencer career.

Embracing Continuous Learning and Adaptation

Embracing continuous learning and adaptation is crucial for staying relevant, growing as an influencer, and thriving in a rapidly evolving landscape. Here are some strategies to help you embrace continuous learning and adaptation:

1. Stay Curious and Open-Minded: Foster a mindset of curiosity and a thirst for knowledge. Be open to new ideas, trends, and perspectives. Seek out learning opportunities and be willing to explore unfamiliar territory.

2. Follow Industry Trends: Stay informed about the latest trends and developments in your niche and the influencer industry as a whole. Keep an eye on emerging platforms, content formats, and audience preferences. This knowledge will help you adapt your strategies and stay ahead of the curve.

3. Engage in Professional Development: Invest in your professional development by attending workshops, webinars, conferences, or industry events. Participate in online courses, certifications, or coaching programs that enhance your skills, knowledge, and understanding of best practices.

4. Learn from Others: Engage with other influencers, thought leaders, and experts in your field. Follow their content, engage in discussions, and learn from their experiences. Collaborate with peers and seek mentorship opportunities to gain insights and expand your perspective.

5. Seek Feedback and Reflection: Regularly seek feedback from your audience, peers, or industry professionals. Reflect on your own performance, content, and strategies. Analyse what's working and what needs improvement. Use feedback as a catalyst for growth and adaptation.

6. Experiment and Innovate: Be willing to experiment with new ideas, content formats, or strategies. Take calculated risks and push the boundaries of your creativity. Embrace innovation and be open to trying new approaches to engage your audience.

7. Embrace Data and Analytics: Utilize data and analytics to gain insights into your audience, content performance, and trends. Analyse metrics such as engagement rates, reach, and audience demographics. Use this information to optimize your content and strategies.

8. Adapt to Platform Changes: Social media platforms and algorithms evolve constantly. Stay updated on platform changes, algorithm updates, and policy guidelines. Adjust your content strategy, distribution methods, and engagement techniques to align with platform requirements.

9. Foster a Learning Community: Surround yourself with a network of fellow influencers or industry professionals who are also committed to continuous learning. Engage in discussions, share insights, and exchange ideas. Collaborate on projects and learn from each other's experiences.

10. Embrace Flexibility and Agility: Be flexible and adaptable in your approach. Embrace change as an opportunity for growth rather than a setback. Stay agile in responding to market shifts, audience preferences, and emerging opportunities.

Remember, learning is a lifelong journey, and adaptation is a key trait of successful influencers. By embracing continuous learning and adaptation, you can stay ahead of the curve, deliver value to your audience, and position yourself as a trusted and influential voice in your niche.

Appendix:

A. Resources and Tools for Influencers
B. Glossary of Key Terms
C. Worksheets and Templates for Planning and Tracking

Note: The contents list provided is a general outline and can be customized or expanded based on the specific focus and requirements of the self-help guidebook.

Appendix A - Resources and Tools for Influencers

As an influencer, there are various resources and tools available to help you enhance your content creation, optimize your workflow, and manage your influencer business effectively. Here are some essential resources and tools for influencers:

Content Creation and Editing:

- Adobe Creative Cloud: Suite of creative tools including Photoshop, Lightroom, Premiere Pro, and Illustrator for professional photo and video editing.
- Canva: User-friendly graphic design platform for creating stunning visuals, social media graphics, and promotional materials.
- VSCO: Photo editing app with a range of filters and editing tools to enhance your images.
- Final Cut Pro or iMovie (for Mac users): Video editing software for creating and editing high-quality videos.
- Audacity: Free audio editing software for recording and editing podcasts or voiceovers.

Social Media Management and Analytics:

- Hootsuite: Social media management platform for scheduling posts, engaging with your audience, and monitoring analytics.
- Buffer: Social media scheduling tool that allows you to plan and schedule posts across multiple platforms.
- Sprout Social: All-in-one social media management and analytics platform to manage, schedule, and analyse your social media presence.
- Google Analytics: Web analytics tool to track and analyse website traffic, audience behaviour, and performance metrics.

Influencer Marketing Platforms:

- Upfluence: Influencer marketing platform that connects brands with influencers and provides campaign management tools.
- AspireIQ: Influencer marketing platform for finding, managing, and measuring influencer collaborations.
- GrapeVine: Influencer marketing platform that connects influencers with brand partnerships and monetization opportunities.
- CreatorIQ: Influencer marketing platform with features for influencer discovery, campaign management, and performance tracking.

Productivity and Organization:

- Trello: Collaborative project management tool for organizing tasks, creating to-do lists, and managing workflows.
- Evernote: Note-taking app for capturing ideas, organizing research, and creating content outlines.
- Google Drive: Cloud storage and collaboration platform for storing and sharing files, documents, and media.

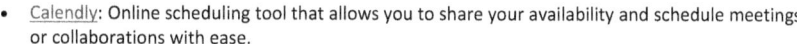

- Calendly: Online scheduling tool that allows you to share your availability and schedule meetings or collaborations with ease.

Learning and Education:

- Udemy: Online learning platform with a wide range of courses on topics like content creation, marketing, photography, and more.
- Skillshare: Platform with thousands of online courses taught by industry professionals, covering various creative and business skills.
- YouTube Creator Academy: Free educational resource specifically for YouTubers, providing tutorials, tips, and best practices for YouTube success.

These are just a few examples of the many resources and tools available to influencers. It's important to explore and find the ones that best suit your needs, budget, and specific goals as an influencer. Regularly evaluate and update your toolkit to stay current with the latest advancements in the industry.

A glossary of key terms commonly used in the context of influencers and influencer marketing:

1. **Affiliate Marketing**: A revenue-sharing model where an influencer promotes a product or service using unique tracking links or codes. They earn a commission for each sale or conversion generated through their affiliate links.
2. **Authenticity**: The quality of being genuine, real, and true to oneself. Authenticity is highly valued in influencer marketing as it helps build trust and credibility with the audience.
3. **Brand Affinity**: The emotional connection and loyalty that an audience has towards a brand as a result of influencer endorsements, content, or brand collaborations. It indicates the effectiveness of influencer marketing in building brand relationships.
4. **Brand Ambassador**: An influencer who develops a long-term relationship with a brand, representing and promoting the brand's values and products/services over an extended period of time.
5. **Brand Collaboration**: A partnership between an influencer and a brand to create content or promote products/services. It typically involves compensation or other benefits for the influencer.
6. **Brand Guidelines**: A set of instructions and specifications provided by a brand to influencers regarding the tone, style, messaging, and visual elements that should be incorporated in the sponsored content to maintain brand consistency.
7. **Call-to-Action (CTA)**: A directive or prompt given by an influencer to their audience, encouraging them to take a specific action, such as visiting a website, making a purchase, or engaging with content.
8. **Content Creator**: A person who produces and publishes various forms of content, such as videos, photos, blogs, or podcasts, with the goal of engaging and entertaining an audience.
9. **Content Strategy**: A plan and approach for creating and distributing content that aligns with the influencer's goals, target audience, and brand identity. It includes content themes, formats, frequency, and distribution channels.
10. **Conversion Rate**: The percentage of audience members who take a desired action, such as making a purchase, signing up for a newsletter, or downloading an app, as a result of an influencer's content or promotion.
11. **Engagement**: The level of interaction and involvement that an influencer's audience has with their content, such as likes, comments, shares, and direct messages.
12. **Engagement Rate**: A measure of the level of engagement an influencer receives on their content, often calculated as a percentage by dividing the total engagements (likes, comments, shares) by the total reach or follower count.
13. **Follower**: A person who chooses to subscribe or follow an influencer's social media accounts or platforms to receive updates and engage with their content.
14. **Impressions**: The number of times an influencer's content has been seen or displayed on a screen. It represents the potential reach of the content, regardless of whether it was interacted with or not.
15. **Influencer**: An individual who has built a dedicated following and possesses the ability to influence the opinions, behaviours, and purchasing decisions of their audience through their online presence and content.

16. **Influencer Agreement**: A legal contract that outlines the terms, expectations, and obligations of both the influencer and the brand in a collaboration. It includes details regarding deliverables, compensation, exclusivity, and intellectual property rights.
17. **Influencer Contract**: A legally binding agreement between an influencer and a brand or advertiser that outlines the terms, expectations, compensation, deliverables, and other relevant details of their collaboration.
18. **Influencer Disclosure**: The requirement for influencers to clearly disclose their partnership, sponsorship, or paid relationship with a brand when promoting or endorsing products or services. It ensures transparency and compliance with advertising regulations.
19. **Influencer Marketing**: A marketing strategy that involves collaborating with influencers to promote products, services, or brands. It leverages the influencers' influence and reach to target and engage their audience.
20. **Influencer Platform**: An online platform or marketplace that connects brands and influencers, facilitating collaboration, campaign management, and influencer discovery. These platforms often provide tools and features to streamline the influencer marketing process.
21. **Influencer Score**: A metric or algorithm-based calculation that assesses the influence and impact of an influencer. It takes into account factors such as reach, engagement, audience demographics, and niche expertise.
22. **Micro-Influencer**: An influencer with a smaller following but highly engaged audience within a specific niche or community. They typically have a more personal connection with their followers.
23. **Niche**: A specific topic, interest, or area of focus that an influencer specializes in and creates content around. It helps them target a specific audience and establish expertise in that particular field.
24. **Reach**: The total number of unique individuals who see an influencer's content or have the potential to see it. It indicates the overall size of an influencer's audience.
25. **ROI (Return on Investment)**: A metric used to measure the effectiveness and profitability of an influencer marketing campaign. It assesses the returns generated compared to the investment made.
26. **ROI Tracking**: The process of measuring and analysing the return on investment from influencer marketing campaigns. It involves tracking key performance indicators (KPIs), such as conversions, sales, website traffic, or brand mentions.
27. **Sponsored Content**: Content created by an influencer in collaboration with a brand or advertiser. The influencer receives compensation, products, or services in exchange for featuring the brand or promoting its products or services to their audience.
28. **Social Listening**: The practice of monitoring and analysing social media conversations, mentions, and sentiment related to an influencer, brand, or specific campaign. It provides insights into audience perception and sentiment.
29. **Sponsored Post**: A social media post created by an influencer as part of a collaboration with a brand or advertiser. It is identified as sponsored or in partnership with the brand.

Remember, the influencer marketing landscape is dynamic and constantly evolving, so new terms and concepts may emerge over time. It's essential to stay updated and continue learning to navigate the industry effectively.

Here are some worksheets and templates that can help you with planning and tracking as an influencer:

Content Calendar Template: Use a content calendar template to plan and organize your content in advance. You can include details such as content ideas, posting dates, platforms, and any collaborations or sponsored content. This helps you stay organized and consistent in your content creation.

Month/Year: [Insert Month/Year]

Platform: [Insert Social Media Platform]

Content Categories:

1. [Insert Content Category 1]
2. [Insert Content Category 2]
3. [Insert Content Category 3]

Date	Content Description	Content Category	Notes
[Insert Date 1]	[Insert Content Description]	[Insert Content Category]	[Insert Notes]
[Insert Date 2]	[Insert Content Description]	[Insert Content Category]	[Insert Notes]
[Insert Date 3]	[Insert Content Description]	[Insert Content Category]	[Insert Notes]

Feel free to customize the template based on your specific needs. You can add or remove columns as necessary, such as including columns for hashtags, captions, or collaborations. Additionally, you can create separate tabs or sheets for each social media platform or month to keep your content calendar organized.

Remember to refer to your content strategy and goals when planning your content. Use this template as a guide to map out your content in advance, ensuring a consistent and well-planned approach to your influencer content creation.

Social Media Analytics Template: Track your social media performance using an analytics template. Include metrics like follower growth, engagement rate, reach, and impressions. Regularly updating this template allows you to monitor your progress and identify areas for improvement.

Platform: [Insert Social Media Platform] **Time Period:** [Insert Time Period, e.g., Month/Quarter/Year]

Metrics to Track:

1. **Followers/Fans:** [Insert Current Number]
2. **Engagement Rate:** [Insert Calculation Formula]
3. **Reach:** [Insert Calculation Formula]
4. **Impressions:** [Insert Calculation Formula]
5. **Top Performing Posts:**
   - Post 1: [Insert Post Description]
   - Post 2: [Insert Post Description]
   - Post 3: [Insert Post Description]
   - Post 4: [Insert Post Description]
   - Post 5: [Insert Post Description]
6. **Audience Demographics:**
   - Age Range: [Insert Age Range]
   - Gender: [Insert Gender Distribution]
   - Location: [Insert Location Distribution]
   - Interests: [Insert Key Interests]
7. **Referral Traffic:** [Insert Key Sources and Percentages]
8. **Content Performance by Category:**
   - Category 1: [Insert Performance Metrics]
   - Category 2: [Insert Performance Metrics]
   - Category 3: [Insert Performance Metrics]
   - Category 4: [Insert Performance Metrics]
   - Category 5: [Insert Performance Metrics]

Feel free to customize the template based on your specific needs and the metrics that are most relevant to your social media platforms. You can add or remove sections, include additional metrics, or modify the layout to fit your requirements.

Regularly update the template with the latest data to track your social media performance, identify trends, and make informed decisions to optimize your content and engagement strategies.

Remember to analyse the data and draw insights from it to improve your social media presence and achieve your influencer goals.

Influencer Campaign Brief Template: When collaborating with brands, use a campaign brief template to outline the campaign objectives, deliverables, guidelines, and key messaging. This helps ensure a clear understanding between you and the brand and serves as a reference throughout the collaboration.

Campaign Brief: [Insert Campaign Name]

Campaign Overview:

- Brand/Client: [Insert Brand/Client Name]
- Campaign Objective: [Insert Campaign Objective]
- Campaign Duration: [Insert Campaign Duration]
- Key Message: [Insert Key Message or Call-to-Action]
- Hashtags: [Insert Campaign Hashtags]

Deliverables:

- Content Types: [Insert Content Types, e.g., Instagram posts, Instagram Stories, blog post]
- Number of Posts: [Insert Number of Posts]
- Post Format: [Insert Post Format, e.g., photo, video, carousel]
- Post Captions: [Insert Caption Guidelines]

Brand Guidelines:

- Brand Voice: [Insert Brand Voice Description]
- Visual Identity: [Insert Brand Colours, Fonts, and Style Guidelines]
- Brand Values: [Insert Key Brand Values]
- Key Messages: [Insert Key Messages to Incorporate]

Content Requirements:

- Product/Service Integration: [Insert Product/Service Details]
- Unique Selling Points: [Insert Key Product/Service Features]
- Call-to-Action: [Insert Desired Call-to-Action]

Timeline:

- Content Creation: [Insert Dates/Timeline for Content Creation]
- Content Submission: [Insert Submission Deadline]
- Campaign Activation: [Insert Campaign Activation Date]
- Reporting: [Insert Reporting Deadline]

Compensation:

- Compensation Details: [Insert Compensation Details or Negotiated Terms]
- Payment Terms: [Insert Payment Terms]

Additional Notes/Guidelines:

- [Insert any additional notes or guidelines provided by the brand/client]

Remember to customize this template based on the specific requirements and guidelines provided by the brand/client for each campaign. The brief should provide clear instructions, expectations, and guidelines to ensure a successful collaboration.

Make sure to address all necessary details, including content types, brand guidelines, key messages, and compensation terms. This template will help both you and the brand/client have a clear understanding of the campaign and deliverables.

Always maintain open communication with the brand/client to clarify any questions or concerns and ensure that both parties are aligned throughout the collaboration.

Expense Tracking Worksheet: Keep track of your expenses related to your influencer business using an expense tracking worksheet. This includes expenses like equipment purchases, software subscriptions, travel costs, and marketing expenses. It helps you manage your finances and stay organized during tax season.

Expense Tracking Worksheet

Date	Expense Description	Category	Amount ($)
[Date]	[Expense Description]	[Expense Category]	[Amount]
[Date]	[Expense Description]	[Expense Category]	[Amount]
[Date]	[Expense Description]	[Expense Category]	[Amount]

Expense Categories:

- Advertising and Promotion
- Equipment and Gear
- Software and Subscriptions
- Travel and Transportation
- Office Supplies
- Professional Services
- Education and Training
- Other

Total Expenses: $ [Total Amount]

Feel free to customize the template based on your specific expense categories and needs. You can add or remove columns as necessary, such as including columns for payment method or tracking tax-related information.

Regularly update the worksheet by adding new expenses as they occur. This will help you keep track of your spending, manage your budget, and have a clear overview of your influencer business expenses.

Consider using expense tracking software or apps that automate the process and make it easier to categorize and analyse your expenses.

Remember to save receipts and documentation for all your expenses to ensure accurate record-keeping and tax compliance.

By regularly tracking your expenses, you'll have a better understanding of your financial situation and can make informed decisions to optimize your spending and maximize your profitability as an influencer.

Partnership Agreement Template: When entering into collaborations or sponsored content agreements, use a partnership agreement template to outline the terms, obligations, compensation, and other details. Having a clear agreement protects both parties and ensures a smooth collaboration.

Partnership Agreement: [Insert Partnership Name]

Parties Involved:

- Influencer: [Insert Influencer Name]
- Brand/Client: [Insert Brand/Client Name]

Effective Date: [Insert Effective Date]

Term of Agreement:

- Start Date: [Insert Start Date]
- End Date: [Insert End Date or Duration of Agreement]

Scope of Partnership:

- Overview: [Provide a brief overview of the partnership objectives and goals]
- Deliverables: [Specify the content or activities expected from the influencer]
- Exclusivity: [Indicate if the partnership includes exclusivity or non-compete clauses]
- Compensation: [Outline the agreed compensation or benefits for the influencer]

Content Guidelines and Approval Process:

- Brand Guidelines: [Provide details on the brand's visual identity, voice, and content requirements]
- Approval Process: [Specify the process for content review and approval]

Ownership and Usage Rights:

- Intellectual Property: [Specify the ownership of content and intellectual property rights]
- Usage Rights: [Outline the brand's rights to use the influencer's content]

Confidentiality and Non-Disclosure:

- Confidentiality: [Specify any confidential information that should be protected]
- Non-Disclosure: [Outline the obligations regarding non-disclosure of confidential information]

Termination and Dispute Resolution:

- Termination: [Outline the conditions or reasons for termination of the partnership]

- Dispute Resolution: [Specify the preferred method of dispute resolution, such as mediation or arbitration]

Indemnification:

- Indemnification Clause: [Outline the responsibilities of each party regarding legal claims or liabilities]

Governing Law and Jurisdiction:

- Governing Law: [Specify the jurisdiction and laws that govern the partnership agreement]

Miscellaneous:

- Amendments: [Specify the process for making amendments to the agreement]
- Entire Agreement: [Indicate that the agreement represents the entire understanding between the parties]

Signatures:

- [Influencer Name]: [Influencer Signature]
- [Brand/Client Name]: [Brand/Client Signature]

Remember to customize this template based on your specific partnership arrangement and consult with legal professionals if necessary to ensure compliance with applicable laws and regulations.

Carefully review and negotiate the terms with the brand/client before signing the agreement to ensure mutual understanding and alignment of expectations.

Having a partnership agreement helps protect the interests of both parties and provides clarity on the rights, responsibilities, and compensation associated with the collaboration.

Goal Setting Worksheet: Use a goal setting worksheet to define your short-term and long-term goals as an influencer. This includes goals related to follower growth, engagement, brand collaborations, monetization, or personal development. Setting clear goals helps you stay focused and motivated.

Goal Setting Worksheet

1. Overall Goal:

- [Insert Your Overall Goal]

2. Short-Term Goals:

- Goal 1: [Insert Short-Term Goal]
    - Specific Objective: [Specify the specific objective or outcome]
    - Deadline: [Insert Deadline]
    - Action Steps: [Outline the action steps needed to achieve the goal]
- Goal 2: [Insert Short-Term Goal]
    - Specific Objective: [Specify the specific objective or outcome]
    - Deadline: [Insert Deadline]
    - Action Steps: [Outline the action steps needed to achieve the goal]

3. Long-Term Goals:

- Goal 1: [Insert Long-Term Goal]
    - Specific Objective: [Specify the specific objective or outcome]
    - Deadline: [Insert Deadline]
    - Action Steps: [Outline the action steps needed to achieve the goal]
- Goal 2: [Insert Long-Term Goal]
    - Specific Objective: [Specify the specific objective or outcome]
    - Deadline: [Insert Deadline]
    - Action Steps: [Outline the action steps needed to achieve the goal]

4. Key Performance Indicators (KPIs):

- KPI 1: [Insert KPI]
    - Target: [Specify the target or benchmark]
    - Measurement Method: [Outline how you will measure the KPI]
- KPI 2: [Insert KPI]
    - Target: [Specify the target or benchmark]
    - Measurement Method: [Outline how you will measure the KPI]

5. Progress Tracking:

- Milestones: [Identify key milestones or checkpoints to measure your progress]
    - Milestone 1: [Specify the milestone and deadline]
    - Milestone 2: [Specify the milestone and deadline]

- Progress Evaluation: [Specify the frequency of progress evaluation and review]

6. Rewards and Celebrations:

- Rewards: [Outline rewards or incentives to celebrate reaching your goals]
  - Reward 1: [Specify the reward or celebration]
  - Reward 2: [Specify the reward or celebration]

7. Reflection and Adjustments:

- Reflection Periods: [Specify the intervals for reflection and reassessment]
- Adjustments: [Outline how you will adjust your goals or strategies based on your reflections]

Remember to customize this template based on your specific goals, timeframes, and objectives. Regularly review and update your goals, action steps, and progress to stay focused and motivated on your influencer journey.

Keep track of your progress and celebrate milestones along the way to maintain motivation and acknowledge your achievements. Periodically reflect on your goals and make adjustments as needed to ensure they align with your evolving aspirations.

By using a goal setting worksheet, you can establish clear objectives, track your progress, and stay accountable to your goals as you work towards success as an influencer.

Content Idea Brainstorming Sheet: Use a brainstorming sheet to jot down content ideas as they come to mind. This can include video concepts, blog post topics, social media challenges, or series ideas. Having a dedicated sheet allows you to capture ideas for future content creation.

Content Idea Brainstorming Sheet

Topic/Niche:

- [Insert Your Topic/Niche]

Content Categories:

1. [Insert Content Category 1]
2. [Insert Content Category 2]
3. [Insert Content Category 3]
4. [Insert Content Category 4]
5. [Insert Content Category 5]

Content Ideas:

Content Category	Content Idea Description
[Insert Category]	[Insert Content Idea]
[Insert Category]	[Insert Content Idea]
[Insert Category]	[Insert Content Idea]
[Insert Category]	[Insert Content Idea]
[Insert Category]	[Insert Content Idea]

Additional Notes:

- [Insert any additional notes or details related to your content ideas]

Feel free to customize this template based on your specific topic or niche and the content categories you want to focus on. You can add or remove rows as needed to accommodate more content ideas.

In the "Content Categories" section, you can identify different types or themes of content that align with your niche. This helps you organize your ideas and ensures variety in your content creation.

In the "Content Ideas" table, list specific content ideas under each category. Be as descriptive as possible to capture the essence of the idea. Feel free to include any related notes or details to provide additional context or inspiration.

Use this sheet to brainstorm content ideas whenever inspiration strikes. It serves as a handy reference to help you plan and create content that resonates with your audience and aligns with your influencer goals.

Remember to regularly update and refine your content idea brainstorming sheet as new ideas emerge and evolve. By maintaining an organized list of content ideas, you'll never run out of inspiration for your influencer content creation.

Collaboration Tracker Template: If you frequently collaborate with brands or other influencers, use a collaboration tracker template to keep track of past and upcoming collaborations. Include details such as brand/influencer name, campaign details, compensation, deadlines, and contact information. This helps you manage your collaborations and ensure timely delivery.

Collaboration Tracker

Brand/Client	Collaboration Type	Collaboration Period	Deliverables	Compensation	Status
[Brand/Client Name]	[Type of Collaboration]	[Collaboration Period]	[Specific Deliverables]	[Compensation Details]	[Status: In Progress/Completed]
[Brand/Client Name]	[Type of Collaboration]	[Collaboration Period]	[Specific Deliverables]	[Compensation Details]	[Status: In Progress/Completed]
[Brand/Client Name]	[Type of Collaboration]	[Collaboration Period]	[Specific Deliverables]	[Compensation Details]	[Status: In Progress/Completed]

Additional Notes:

- [Insert any additional notes or details related to each collaboration]

Feel free to customize this template based on your specific needs and the information you want to track for each collaboration. You can add or remove columns as necessary to include additional information, such as contact details, campaign objectives, or specific dates.

In the table, include columns for the brand/client name, collaboration type (e.g., sponsored post, brand ambassadorship), collaboration period, specific deliverables, compensation details, and status of each collaboration. The "Status" column allows you to easily track whether the collaboration is in progress or completed.

In the "Additional Notes" section, you can add any relevant details or specific requirements for each collaboration.

Regularly update the Collaboration Tracker as new collaborations arise or progress. It helps you stay organized, manage timelines and deliverables, and ensures you maintain clear communication with the brands/clients you collaborate with.

By using a Collaboration Tracker, you can easily track and manage your collaborations, ensuring timely delivery of content and proper compensation.

Audience Demographics Worksheet: Gain a better understanding of your audience by creating an audience demographics worksheet. Collect data on their age range, gender, location, interests, and other relevant information. This helps you tailor your content to better serve your audience's preferences.

Audience Demographics Worksheet

Social Media Platform: [Insert Social Media Platform] **Time Period:** [Insert Time Period, e.g., Month/Quarter/Year]

Demographic Categories:

1. Age Range
2. Gender
3. Location
4. Interests
5. Other relevant categories

Demographic Data:

Demographic Category	Audience Percentage
Age Range	[Percentage]
Gender	[Percentage]
Location	[Percentage]
Interests	[Percentage]
Other	[Percentage]

Key Insights:

- [Insert Key Insights or Observations about your audience demographics]

Additional Notes:

- [Insert any additional notes or details related to your audience demographics]

Feel free to customize this template based on your specific social media platform and the demographic categories that are relevant to your audience. You can add or remove rows and categories as needed.

In the "Demographic Data" table, record the percentage or proportion of your audience for each demographic category. This data can be obtained from social media analytics tools or platforms that provide audience insights.

In the "Key Insights" section, jot down any observations or key insights you gather from analysing your audience demographics. This could include patterns, trends, or characteristics that stand out.

The "Additional Notes" section allows you to add any relevant notes or details about your audience demographics that may be valuable for future content planning or audience targeting.

Regularly update this worksheet to reflect changes in your audience demographics over time. This helps you tailor your content and engagement strategies to better meet the needs and preferences of your audience.

By understanding your audience demographics, you can create content that resonates with your target audience and develop strategies to grow and engage your follower base more effectively.

Monthly Analytics Review Template: Conduct a monthly analytics review using a template that allows you to analyse your social media and website metrics. This helps you identify trends, measure progress towards your goals, and make data-driven decisions for future content strategies:

Monthly Analytics Review: [Insert Month/Year]

Platform: [Insert Social Media Platform/Website]

Key Metrics:

1. **Follower/Fan Growth:**
   - Starting Followers/Fans: [Insert Starting Number]
   - Ending Followers/Fans: [Insert Ending Number]
   - Net Growth: [Insert Net Growth]
2. **Engagement Rate:**
   - Average Engagement Rate: [Insert Average Engagement Rate]
   - Engagement Rate Comparison to Previous Month: [Insert Comparison, e.g., Increased/Decreased by X%]
3. **Top Performing Posts/Content:**
   - Post/Content 1: [Insert Description or Key Metrics]
   - Post/Content 2: [Insert Description or Key Metrics]
   - Post/Content 3: [Insert Description or Key Metrics]
   - Post/Content 4: [Insert Description or Key Metrics]
   - Post/Content 5: [Insert Description or Key Metrics]
4. **Website Traffic:**
   - Total Website Visits: [Insert Total Visits]
   - Traffic Sources: [Insert Key Traffic Sources and Percentages]
   - Bounce Rate: [Insert Bounce Rate]
   - Conversion Rate: [Insert Conversion Rate]
5. **Audience Demographics:**
   - Age Range: [Insert Age Range Distribution]
   - Gender: [Insert Gender Distribution]
   - Location: [Insert Location Distribution]
   - Interests: [Insert Key Interests]

Highlights and Insights:

- [Insert Key Highlights or Insights from the Analytics Review]

Areas for Improvement:

- [Identify any areas for improvement or opportunities for growth]

Action Plan for Next Month:

- [Outline specific actions or strategies to implement based on the insights gained]

Additional Notes:

- [Insert any additional notes or details related to the analytics review]

Feel free to customize this template based on the specific social media platforms or website analytics you track, and the metrics that are most relevant to your goals and objectives.

Regularly conduct a monthly analytics review to analyse your performance, identify trends, and gain insights into your audience and content strategies. Use this template to document your findings and plan actionable steps to improve your influencer presence.

By regularly reviewing your analytics, you can make data-driven decisions, optimize your content strategies, and better understand the preferences and behaviours of your audience.

Feel free to customize and adapt these templates to fit your specific needs as an influencer. They can serve as helpful tools for planning, tracking, and staying organized throughout your influencer journey.

If you have further questions on topics or see an opportunity for more inclusions in this publication, please feel free to email us and we will investigate it for the next edition. If your idea is included, we will note you as a contributor for that piece as well as provide you with a free copy of the updated edition.